# CLOSE-QUARTERS COMBAT FOR POLICE AND SECURITY FORCES

## BY ROBERT K. SPEAR

**To all my students, past present, and future; and to my supporting family. Thanks!**

## UNIVERSAL FORCE DYNAMICS

410 DELAWARE
LEAVENWORTH, KANSAS 66048
(913) 682-6518

ISBN 0-9622627-4-9
Library of Congress Catalog Number:

## DISCLAIMER

Please note that the publisher of this instructional book is **NOT RESPONSIBLE** in any manner whatsoever for any injury which may occur by reading and/or following the instructions herein.

It is essential that before following any of the activities, physical or otherwise, herein described, the reader or readers should first consult his or her physician for advice on whether or not the reader or readers should embark on the physical activity described herein. Since the physical activities described herein may be too sophisticated in nature, it is *essential that a physician be consulted.*

Typesetting, design, and photography:
Robert K. Spear

# ACKNOWLEDGEMENTS

The author is especially grateful to the two models who so willingly sacrificed time away from their famililies to assist with this project. A little needs to be said about their backgrounds to convey how special their help was.

**U.S. Army SPC Steven W. Gooler Jr. :**
A Military Security Policeman for the U.S. Army 66th Military Intelligence Brigade, Steve has attended such schools as:

- Protective Services Defense School
- Emergency Medical Technician
- Terrorist Evasive Driving School

**U.S. Army Staff Sergeant Michael Anthony (Tony) DeForrest:**
Also an MP for the 66th MI Bde, Tony has attended such schools as:

- First Responder Course
- Protective Services Defense School
- Terrorist Evasive Driving School
- Unarmed Self Defense
- Artic Survival School

Both of these soldiers have served as full-time bodyguards for the 66th MI Brigade Commander as well as for dignitaries to include: numerous U.S. Ambassadors, the Supreme Commander Europe, the Commander-In-Chief U.S. Army Europe and 7th Army, the Secretary of the Army, and the Secretary of Defense for International Security Policy.

In case the reader wonders, Steve was the security officer and Tony was the assailant in the pictures throughout this book and on its cover.

# ABOUT THE AUTHOR

A fifth-degree black belt, Mr. Spear is considered an American pioneer in the Korean street fighting art of Hapkido. In 1975, he was the first American to attain a third degree black belt and instructor's certification in Korea. He is the chairman of the United States Hapkido Federation's Board of Examiners and is a member of the Midori Yama Budokai Association.

A former U.S. Army Intelligence officer, Mr. Spear has taught combat fighting and self-defense to soldiers, security forces, and civilians in Korea, the United States, and Europe since 1974.

An internationally recognized martial arts theorist and author, Mr. Spear has presented papers to such bodies as the 1984 and 1988 Olympic Scientific Congresses. He has been published in international scientific journals and several martial art and military magazines. His previous books include:

- **Survival On the Battlefield: A Handbook to Military Martial Arts**

- **Hapkido: The Integrated Fighting Art**

- **Surviving Hostage Situations (with Maj. D. Michael Moak)**

A devoted family man, Mr. Spear resides in Leavenworth, KS, where he works as a consultant, a bookstore owner, a publisher, and is the Deputy for the U.S. Army Training and Doctrine Command's Program Integration Office for Deception Operations.

# TABLE OF CONTENTS

# CHAPTER 1

# INTRODUCTION

It was the summer of 1988 that I heard these gratifying words, "It worked, Mr. Spear, it worked just like you said it would!" This statement came from the lips of a young military policeman who had attended a two-hour workshop on close-quarters combat for security forces which I had presented to his section the previous winter. Every summer the Munich American community puts on the "Little Oktober Fest" to raise money for various worthy causes in the area. Large crowds of over 3-5 thousand people are attracted to the carnival rides, booths, good beer, food, and music. With all the booze flowing, sometimes people will get a bit rowdy.

This young PFC and his partner had been assigned a roving security mission. Essentially they were beat cops. The reason the young soldier was so excited was because they had chanced upon a drunk who was beating his girlfriend and attempting to rip her clothes off in full view of the fest crowds. The MP came up to him from behind and grabbed his shoulder to spin him around. The drunk came around swinging, and be-cause they were too close and because there was a crowd all around them, the MP didn't have enough room to reach his right hand across his body to withdraw his nightstick. Without even thinking about it, he executed a left-handed-draw-and-poke to the assailant's solar plexus. (This technique is described in Chapter 2: The Proper Use of the Nightstick, and is not generally taught at the MP School). His assailant immediately collapsed to the ground, gagging. Bingo, the fight was over. The MPs cuffed him and walked him over to the security office to turn him over to the German Polizei.

A professional trainer seldom gets feedback like this from his ex-students. Especially gratifying was that he had instinctively remembered a technique from a training session he'd had months ago with zero reinforcement. In my experience as a part-time self-defense trainer since 1974, I have rarely seen security personnel who could be considered highly trained in close-quarters fighting. They are generally given excellent periodic firearms training; however, most of their hand-to-hand expertise comes from a week or two of academy training, from what they learn on their own at karate schools, or (most dangerously for them) from what they learn on the streets the hard way.

This shouldn't be a surprise to anyone. Declining police and security force budgets are hard-pressed to provide much beyond the basics for a lot of things these days. Unlike the Japanese police departments, which provide a self-defense work-out gym in every police station, our administrations tend to focus on the sidearm as the preferred response to too many situations. In these days of excessive-force lawsuits, it might behoove administrations to pay more training attention to alternative responses to the close-quarters threat. This is especially important when one considers how often situations arise which disallow the use of a firearm, i.e. in dense crowds, in situations that evolve too quickly to allow the drawing and firing of a sidearm, and for those instances when a firearm hasn't been issued.

Over time, it became apparent that a training guide was needed which incorporated good street sense and the most effective methods taken from up-to-date martial arts developments. Based on a great deal of research and discussions with military, municipal police, and commercial security forces, the following is a manual that covers many of the oft-neglected aspects of close-quarters defense. It purposely does not focus on hand-cuffing and marksmanship techniques since these have been adequately covered by a large body of readily available training literature. One should understand that the enclosed techniques barely scratch the surface when compared to the tremendous pool of possible techniques from which these were drawn. These, however, are some of the simpler yet more effective ones. They are easy to teach, easy to learn, and are geared for both women and men (in other words, they're not strength dependent).

This book is designed as a ready reference that can be used by a security trainer as a training manual or by the individual student as a study guide. These techniques should be practiced until they become second nature. It helps to train with different sized partners and ones of different sexes. Realism, practicality, and professionalism should always be emphasized.

# CHAPTER 2

# PROPER USE OF THE NIGHTSTICK

One of the most effective weapons carried by most security guards is the nightstick. In well-trained hands, it can be used in a wide variety of situations with varying levels of response which range from mildly incapacitating to deadly force. Unlike the Okinawan-based tonfa or PR-24, the nightstick is simple to learn, taking far fewer training hours to attain proficiency. We will present material on the following aspects of the nightstick:

- **The Nightstick**
- **Carrying & Stance**
- **Drawing**
- **Common Mistakes**
- **Effective Targets**
- **Blocking**
- **Poking**
- **Striking**
- **Leverage**
- **Serial Movements**

## The Nightstick

The usual nightstick is approximately two feet long. Most are made out of pine, (a softer wood), as a safety feature. The idea is the stick will break or shatter if it is used against a person's head (which most communities consider excessive force). Some are provided with lanyards and some aren't. The lanyard is controversial. It can be used to reinforce the grip on the stick or as a temporary handcuff. On the other hand, if worn incorrectly (and it usually is), it can be dangerous to its user since it might tie his hand to the stick when the stick is grabbed by an assailant. Although my personal preference is for the 12" hardwood billyclub because it's faster and useful in certain Hapkido stick techniques, it's rather uncommon so it won't be covered by this book. The Maglite flashlight, on the other hand will be addressed because of its effectiveness as a weapon, as a tool, and its common use by police and security forces.

# Carrying & Stance

Since the primary weapon of the security officer is considered to be the sidearm, it is generally worn on the same side as the guard's preferred hand, i.e. a right-handed person will wear the gun on the right side. This leaves the opposite side for the wearing of the nightstick. Although it is usually holstered in a metal ring, occasionally it may be thrust through a belt.

The proper way to stand with the stick is either:

**2. With the stick held back along the arm which is slightly forward. This is used for off-side blocks and strikes**

**1. With the stick held in a hammer grip, hand slightly back, and off-side hand out to guard.**

**3. Both hands gripping each end for blocking or springing strikes.**

# Drawing

There are three methods of drawing the stick.

1. The cross-handed draw is most common.

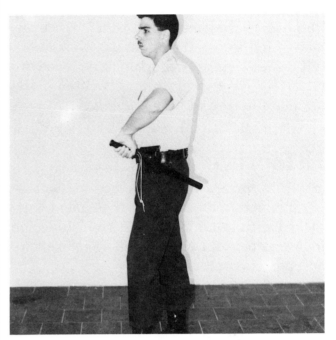

3. If the officer's arm is long enough, this same-sided draw can be executed to place the stick in a normal grip in case the strong-side arm is otherwise engaged.

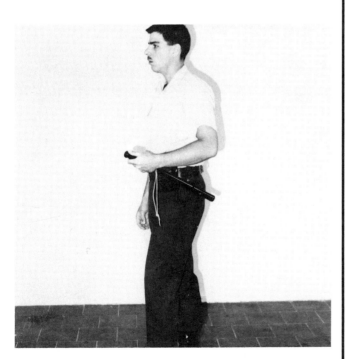

2. The same-side-hand draw is useful.

# Common Mistake

Too many people see sticks as clubs, bludgeoning instruments. They aren't really; they're extensions of the users' arms. Because of this mistaken belief, however, many tend to use the nightstick with large, full-armed swings. Unfortunately, these are relatively easy to block and counter if the assailant knows what he's doing.

# Effective Targets

There are numerous non-lethal vulnerable points on the body that may be attacked with great effect. These include the following points. Note the effects of a strike or a poke to them:

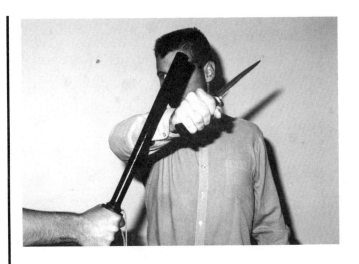

**2. OUTER WRIST: strike causes severe pain and weakness in the grip.**

**3. INSIDE ELBOWS: strike or block causes electric-like shock, pain followed by numbness.**

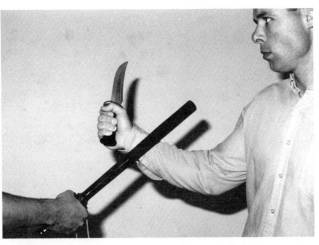

**1. INNER WRIST: a strike causes the hand to release and a hurting numbness remains.**

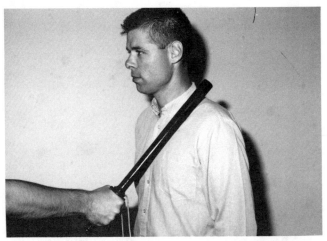

**4. COLLAR BONES: strike can cause severe pain and can break the bone to take away the use of the same-side arm.**

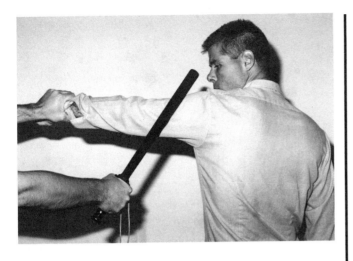

5. BACK OF ARM (TRICEP): strike causes weakness and pain.

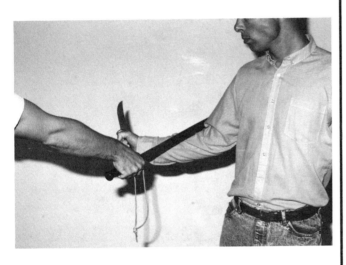

6. FOREARM: strike causes grip release and severe pain and weakness.

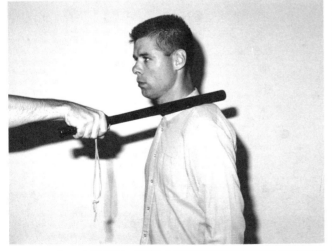

7. SHOULDER (TRAPEZIUS/DELTOID REGION): strike causes pain and general numbing of whole arm.

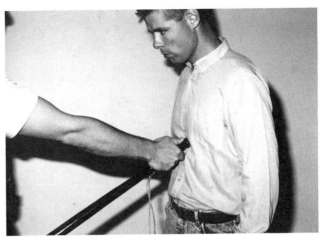

8. SOLAR PLEXUS: poke paralyzes breathing momentarily.

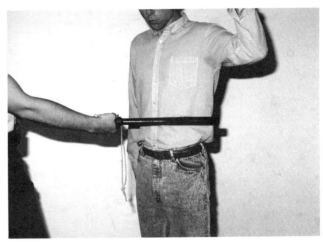

9. SHORT RIBS: poke or strike knocks out breath and hurts.

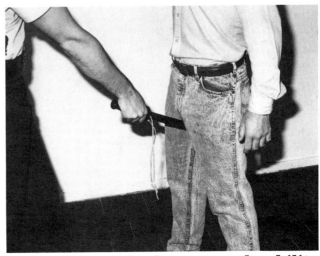

10. GROIN: strike devastates the ability to even think of moving.

7

**11. OUTSIDE OF KNEE:** strike sends electric-like shock throughout leg and causes excruciating pain. Most strikes to any part of the knee will cause it to collapse.

**12. INSIDE OF KNEE:** same

**13. BACK OF KNEE:** same

**14. HAMSTRINGS:** strike will cause paralysis, cramping, and collapse of the leg.

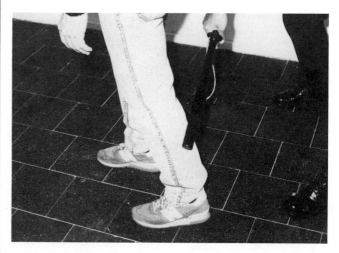

**15. CALF:** strike will cause paralysis and cramping of the lower leg.

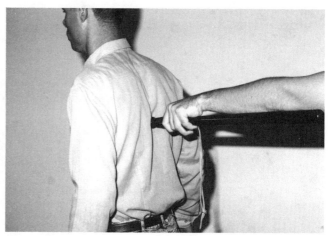

**16. BACK:** strike will cause pain, poke will be excruciating.

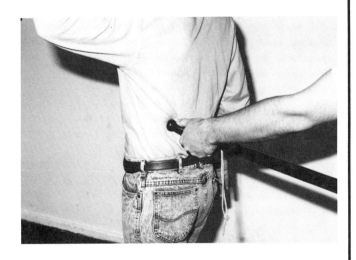

**17. KIDNEYS: same as back**

**18. ANKLE: strike will cause unbearable pain and difficulty in standing.**

**19. HAND: strike will cause grip release, pain, and weakness.**

# Blocking

The nightstick can be used to block blows, kicks, weapon attacks, or to gain more working room. Never use a one-handed hammer-grip block unless you are using a strike as a block. Otherwise, the assailant's blow might carry on through.

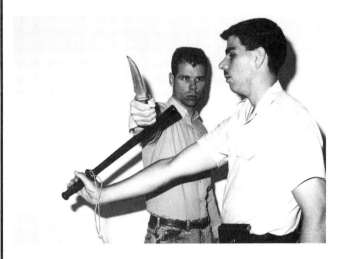

**1. Improper one-handed block.**

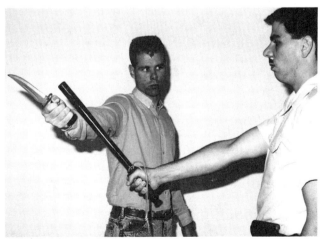

**2. Using a strike to block**

3. Two-handed block to one side and....

5. Rising block.

4. To the other side.

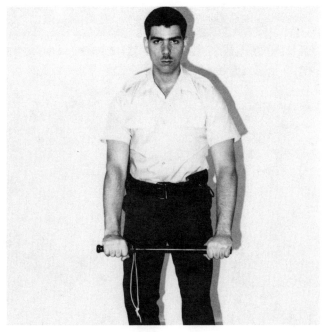

6. Downward block.

7. Off-side-grip block.

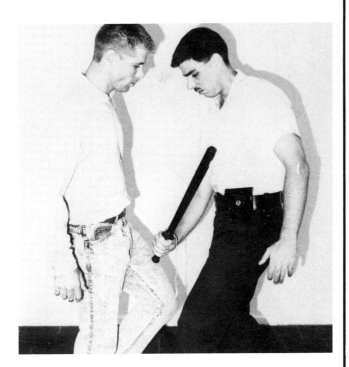

8. Butt-strike block.

9. Pushaway block.

# Poking

This is one of the most effective ways of using the stick. Pokes are fast, devastating, and difficult to block.

1. Straight-on one-handed poke to the body.

2. Two-handed poke to the body.

1. Sometimes it is necessary to draw and poke at the same time. If you don't have room or time to do a cross-body draw, clasp the stick and....

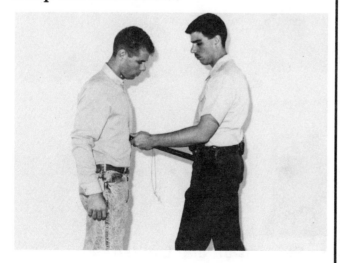

2. Deliver a straightline draw and butt poke into your assailant's solar plexus.

1. If attacked from behind, you don't even need to draw it all the way out, just push the stick forward in the ring and....

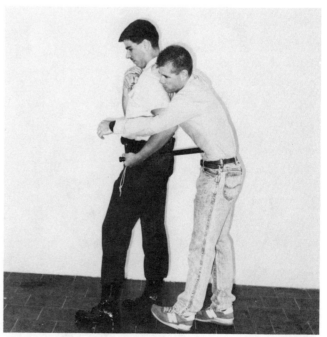

2. Slam its point back into his body.

# Striking

The proper method of striking with the nightstick is with lots of wrist snap. Much more force can be generated much more quickly with a good wrist-snapping strike. These strikes are more difficult to block and are harder to detect. Because the wrist snaps the stick, the motion is more circular. You can also use the butt of the weapon to strike at vulnerable points. Finally, you can strike with the stick laid back along your arm if you have to draw it with a same-sided grip.

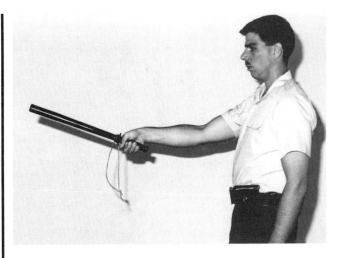

3. Snap it forward with the wrist, allowing the arm to carry it to the target.

1. From the starting position....

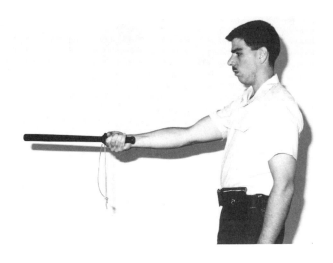

4. The stick can be snapped with a forehand motion, or a....

2. Allow the stick to rock back and....

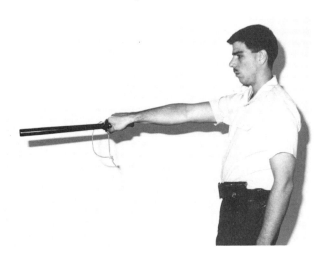

5. Backhand motion.

13

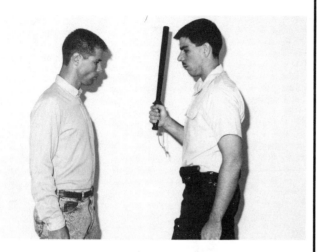

1. The butt can be snapped....

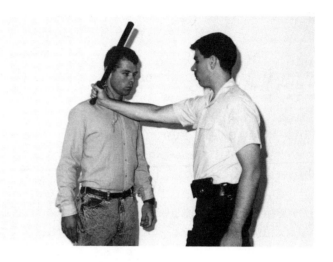

4. Hammered down.

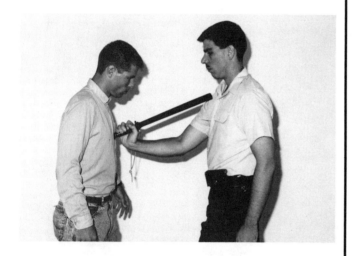

2. Forward into the body or....

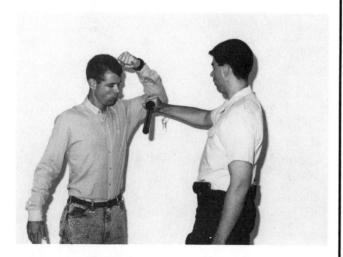

3. Back-handed or....

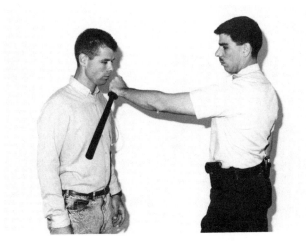

1. The same-sided grip strikes are used when doing a draw-and-strike or draw-and-poke. Here we see a forehand,....

2. A backhand,....

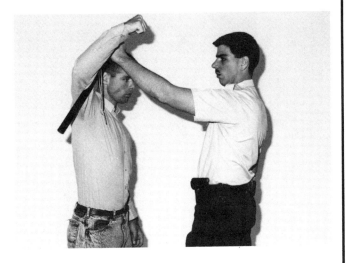

3. And an uppercut.

# Leverage

One of the distinct advantages of the nightstick is its ability to be used as a lever. As an extension of the arm, it can be very helpful. It can be used to:

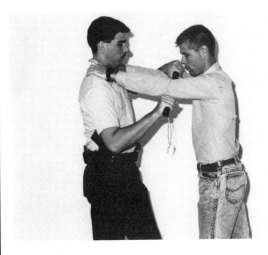

1. Release a....

2. Choke.

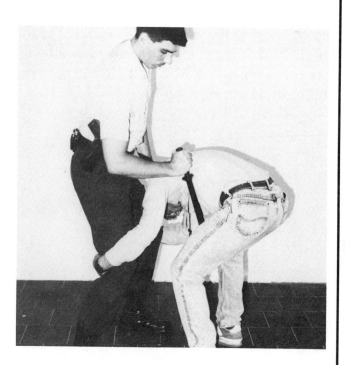

3.  Disrupt a....

5.  Or, increase the pain of a come-along.

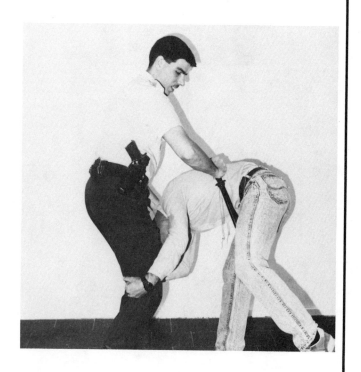

4.  Tackle.

# Serial Movements

A key aspect of close-quarters combat is to never expect one movement or counter-attack to finish the job. You will have a better chance of surviving if you keep the pressure on with multiple, serial attacks until your assailant is no longer able to resist your control. The nightstick is an excellent weapon for this kind of approach. When you strike with a wrist snap, the stick tends to rebound back. This sets up the next strike, then the next. The same thing can be done from one type of a maneuver to another. For instance, you can block, then poke, then strike, then lock up a come-along.

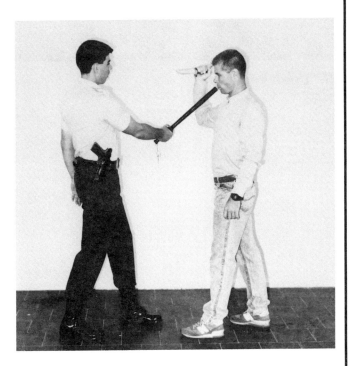

**1. You can strike-block a knife attack, then....**

**2. Strike his knee,....**

**3. His other arm, and....**

**4. His shoulder so that he is incapable of attacking anymore.**

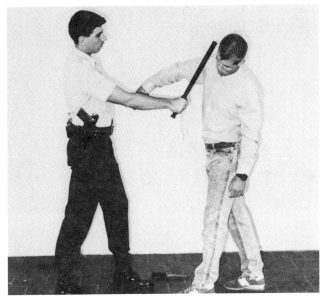

1. You can two-handed block a club attack,....

3. Lock him up.

2. Butt strike his short-ribs, and ....

# MAGLITE USE

The 3-cell metal flashlight is essentially a lead-weighted billy club while the longer version is more like a nightstick. Either can be extremely effective as weapons. First, they obviously are heavy and strong. It's difficult to damage them, while most nightsticks are purposely designed to break as a safety precaution. They are multi-purposed, i.e. they are both a light and a weapon. For these reasons, many officers prefer carrying them instead of a stick. The 3-celled version is used in the following pictures to illustrate how best to use this wonderfully versatile tool. Use it in the same way you would a stick, but remain aware that it is considerably more lethal than a stick.

2. When walking in a confined area, hold the light in a forehand grip at shoulder level. Your finger can press the light switch button to temporarily blind the assailant while....

1. When using both the light and a gun in a dark, wide-open area, carry the light out away from your body. If an assailant fires at your light, there is less chance of you getting hit. You, however, will be able to fire at his pistol flashes.

3. The light clubs down to take him out.

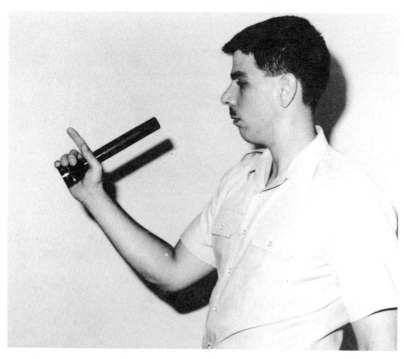

1. The proper way to grip the Maglite is to hold the light with your little finger resting on its reflector housing. This allows you to....

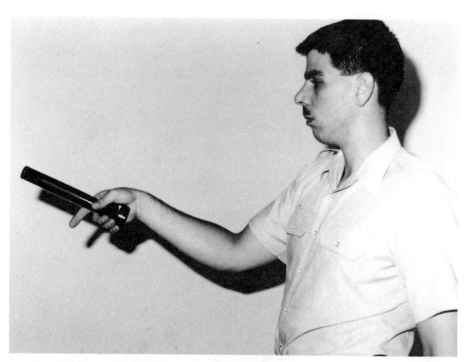

2. Pull the light around, pivoting your hand to deliver a blow.

# CHAPTER 3

# COME-ALONGS

Sometimes it's necessary to move an assailant from one location to another. If you don't have handcuffs or if the situation requires you to move him immediately, the use of a come-along is advised. The ideal come-along renders the assailant relatively helpless by creating severe pain, by placing him off-balance, by tying up his limbs, or by combining any and all of these conditions.

Some of the ones presented here use the nightstick as an aid, some use only the body, and some can be executed either way. It's important to practice these over and over with training partners of differing sizes and sex so their use becomes automatic and they can be adjusted to fit the situation instinctively.

# The Devil's Handshake

1. Clasp his hand in a handshake grip.

2. Pull him sharply toward you to hyperextend his arm. Quickly bring up your free arm under his elbow joint and grasp his opposite shoulder.

3. Lever his hand and fingers down and back while you press up against his elbow with your other arm. It's amazing how fast he'll come up on his tiptoes to escape the pain. This is a good technique for security personnel working parties or bars since it starts out with a friendly handshake.

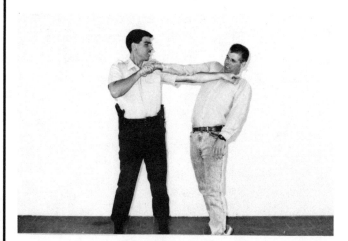

4. A nasty modification is to press your fingertips into his subclavian pressure point and grasp his collar bone. This is unbelievably painful and can be used as a fallback technique if he insists on fighting the Devil's Handshake.

# Near-Side Devil's Handshake

1. This version starts by clasping your assailant in a handshake or by grabbing his wrist and pulling his arm straight.

2. Bring your free arm up under his elbow and slip your hand behind his neck, forcing his head down.

3. Put downward and backward pressure on his hand or wrist which puts strain on his wrist, elbow, and neck. If he still wants to fight, grab his hair on the side of his head and really lock him up.

4. This same technique can be executed with the nightstick by placing it along-side his neck and under his tricep.

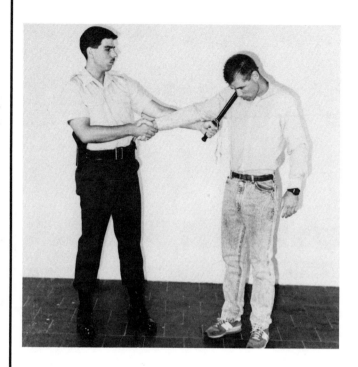

5.   Lever down and press up.

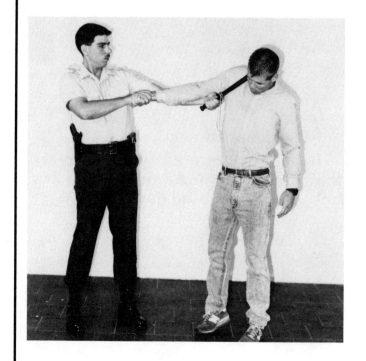

# Citizen's Arrest / Gooseneck

1. Grab his hand with your cross-side hand, i.e. your right hand grabs his right hand. At the same time, reach under his arm, digging your fingertips into the lower end of his bicep near his elbow and

3. Step to his side, bringing his elbow firmly against your body. Release your grip on his bicep and transfer it onto his hand to support your other hand's grip there. Bend his wrist inward and down. This puts intolerable pain on his wrist. If he tries to attack you with his free hand, crank on more pressure to your wrist lock which should quickly discourage him. This is a good come-along for partners to use on both sides of an assailant.

2. ...pull him sharply toward yourself while you push his hand up and away.

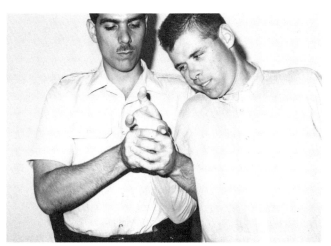

4. A modification is to grab one or two of his middle fingers and bend them the opposite direction as you pull him into position.

# Carotid Lock-up

1. Grab his wrist with your cross-body hand and yank him off balance so that you end up standing behind his shoulder.

while pulling your thumb tendon against his neck pressure point. This puts strain on his elbow, his shoulder, and on his neck. You can also put this on a person who is kneeling to get them up onto his feet.

2. Open your free hand wide apart and bring it around in front of his head, placing the hardened tendon at the base of your thumb against his carotid artery.

3. Pull his arm out straight and back

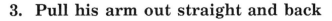

26

# Hammer/Wrist Lock

1. Grab his same-side wrist and pull from behind his elbow with your cross-side hand to spin him around.

2. Push his arm up behind his back and slip your wrist grip into a wrist lock. Push up on his arm and back on his wrist and forward on his body to move him along.

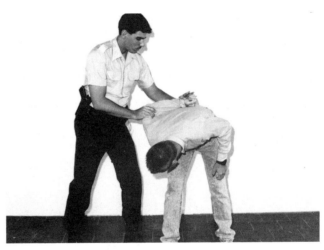

3. Remember to keep your head down and behind his shoulder-blade so he can't attack it with his free hand.

# Full-Nelson Series

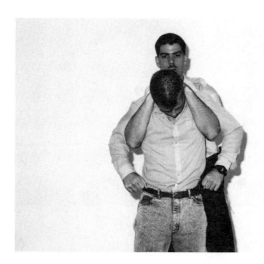

1.  A Full-Nelson is a good backward moving come-along.

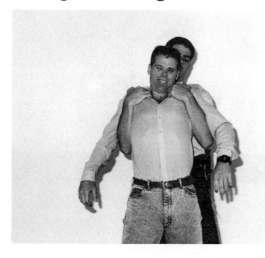

2.  Even better is this painful modification where you grasp both his collar bones and pull down. His reaction will be extreme. Often he'll want to collapse to get away from the pain. This works great with a partner who picks up the assailant's feet so that you can carry him away. If he fights too hard, a good sharp outward yank should break his collar bones, taking away his ability to use his arms. This may be helpful in handling an "Angel-Dusting" berserker.

# Elbow Lock

1.  This come-along works well for one or two security officers. In fact, any of these techniques which isolate to one side of the assailant's body are good candidates for double-teaming which is important when dealing with especially violent subjects. Grab his wrist or hand cross-bodied and yank his arm straight.

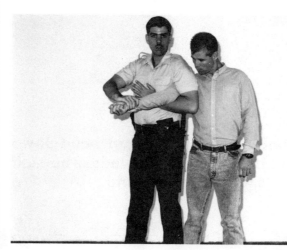

2.  Step to his side and place his upper arm under your armpit while you wedge your lower arm under his elbow.

3. Widely open your hand to harden your forearm and draw it up. At the same time, lever his hand down and back.

5. Lever up with the stick against his elbow while you put downward pressure on his wrist.

4. This is a good technique for use with the nightstick. You start the same way then bring the stick under his elbow and place the end of it on top of your forearm.

# Crotch Roust

1. This stick technique (and I might add that it works better with the billy club or Maglite) is excellent for marching a rowdy out of a room or an area. It produces a feeling of helplessness and total imbalance. Grab him by the collar or the back of the neck while you insert your arm between his legs from the rear, holding your stick at its center.

2. Slam your wrist bones up into his crotch and turn the stick horizontal with your fingers facing upward. Maintaining your grip, pull up on the stick and push his head or neck forward. He either marches forward or ends up flat on his face.

# Wrist Lock

1. Reach cross-body and grab over to the outside edge of his hand.

2. As you pull him toward you, join both your hands in a tandem, mutually re-enforcing grip with your fingers gripping the outside edges of his hand and your thumbs applying pressure to the back of his hand.

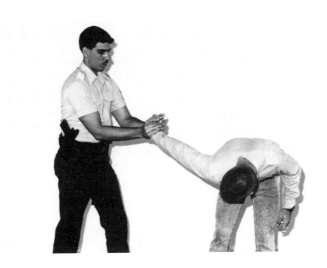

3. Pull him toward you while levering back on his hand. This technique is good for initial control, and it's easy to move into other come-alongs from this one.

# Chicken-Wing / Hair-Pull

1.  While standing alongside the assailant, drive your arm under his arm and up to his shoulder.

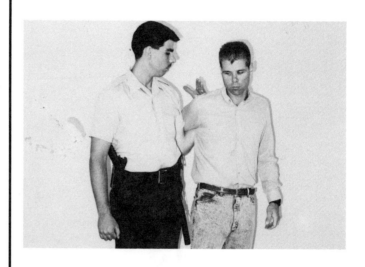

2.  At the same time, reach behind his head and grab his far-side hair. This opposing-directions strain will put him into a terrible bind.

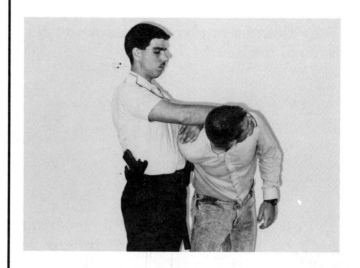

# CHAPTER 4

# UNARMED ATTACKS

If an unarmed assailant attacks you, should you use deadly force? Well, maybe, if he's high on "Angel Dust" (PCP). Otherwise, you are going to have to use an appropriate level of response which means your own body or your nightstick. Now, you're not being asked to go 10 rounds with this character; however, you do have to contain his violence and bring him under control as expeditiously as possible. If you're lucky enough to be a Federal Prison officer who has attended their special Aikido training, you'll have the necessary skills to do this. Unfortunately, Aikido is a very complicated and passive art which takes considerable training hours to master.

So what are you going to do? Again, you have your nightstick and you have your body. For these reasons, we will provide at least one technique from each aspect for each of our threat scenarios which will include:

- **Front choke**

- **Rear choke**

- **Side headlock**

- **Front headlock**

- **Knee to groin**

- **Front Kick to Groin**

- **Kick to knee**

- **Sidekick to body or head**

- **Roundhouse kick**

- **Push to chest**

- **Arm or shoulder grab**

- **Haymaker punch**

- **Boxer's jabs**

- **Tackle**

- **Front bear-hug around the arms**

- **Rear bear-hug around the arms**

These are the sixteen most common threats. There exist thousands of countering techniques which could be used; however, the ones to be presented here are very reliable and don't require many hours of training. Many are similar and very logical in their movements. All techniques should end with you applying a come-along or handcuffs to control and ready him for transport to a secure facility.

# Front Choke
## STICK DEFENSE:

2. Bring your stick over his arms and grab both ends.

1. As the assailant commences his choke, drop your chin and harden your neck to lessen the effects of the choke so you have time to....(This will hold true for all choke releases.)

3. Slam the stick with a snapping motion onto the attacker's forearms which will numb his hands.

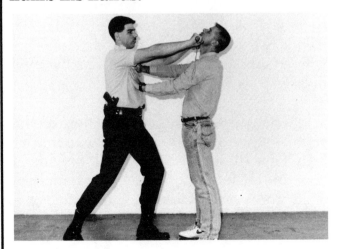

4. Immediately snap the stick back up into his face while stepping forward.

**UNARMED DEFENSE:**

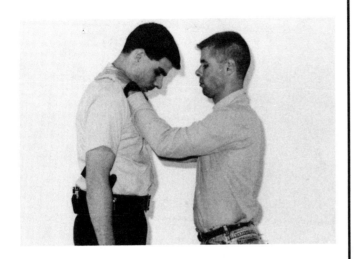

1. Step forward (or back, depending which direction will give you more room to maneuver), and swing your arm across....

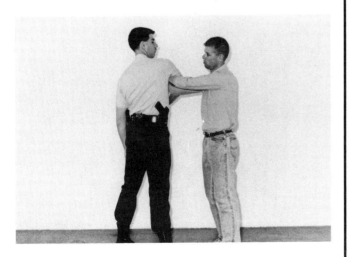

2. His arms, thereby breaking his grip with your body weight and....

3. Reverse your body to strike the assailant in the face with a back-fist.

# Rear Choke

1. Pull your stick forward in its ring holder and....

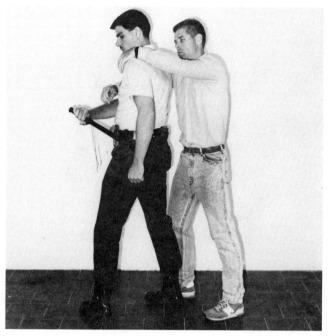

3. As you begin to pivot out of his loosened choke, draw your stick and....

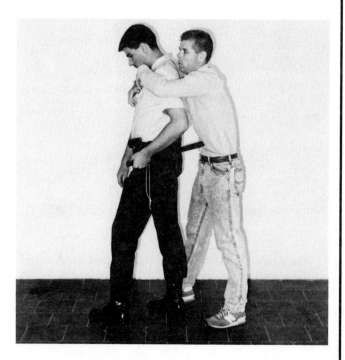

2. Slam its end back into his midsection.

4. Strike the side of his knee.

## UNARMED DEFENSE:

1. Bring your arm forward, hardening it by opening your hand as wide as it will go.

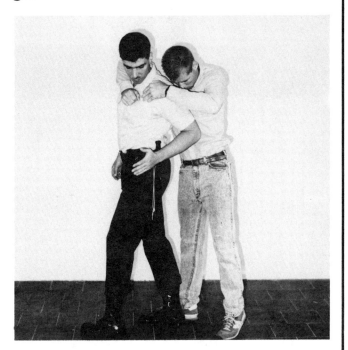

2. Slam your elbow back into his solar plexis or ribs and....

3. Stomp on his foot.

# Side Headlock

## STICK DEFENSE:

1. Crack him across his shins then....

2. Slam your stick and hand back into his groin.

## UNARMED DEFENSE:

1. As he grabs you,....

2. Claw back into his face and....

3. Dump him backwards onto his head.

# Front Headlock

1. Snap your hand and stick up into his groin.

2. As he releases you so that he can put his hands on a more immediate problem. Straighten him up with a two-handed rising block to his face or chest.

1. When he applies the front choke, upper-cut into his groin and....

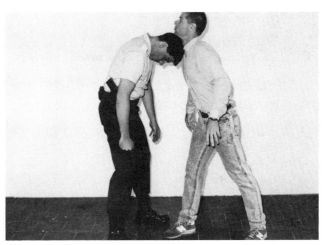

2. Snap your head up into his face to straighten him up.

# Knee to Groin

1. Snap the butt of the stick down and over to charlie-horse his quadracep.

1. As the assailant attempts to knee you in the groin....

2. Step back execute a strike to the side of his supporting knee. This should put him down.

2. Jam and deflect it to the outside with your own knee.

# Front Kick to Groin

1. As he prepares to kick, switch to a two-handed grip. Deflection block his leg (this will be fairly painful for him).

2. Strike his other knee.

41

# UNARMED DEFENSE:

1. As he kicks,....

3. Use a deflection block to allow it to pass by.

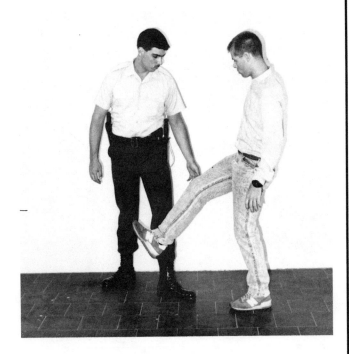

2. Step slightly outside and....

# Kick to Knee

## STICK DEFENSE:

1. As he begins his kick.....

2. Unweight from your front leg while you....

3. Snap a strike into his leg.

## UNARMED DEFENSE:

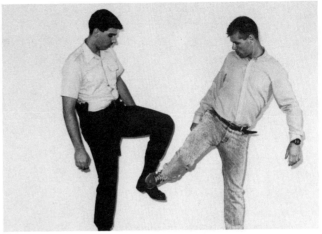

1. As he kicks, raise your front leg up to cover and jam his kick.

# Sidekick to Body or Head

## STICK DEFENSE:

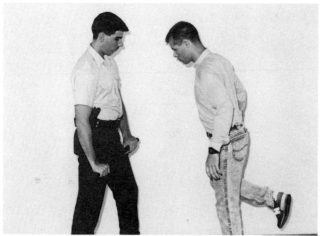

1. As he begins his kick, switch to a two-handed grip and....

2. Deflect the kick with a block.

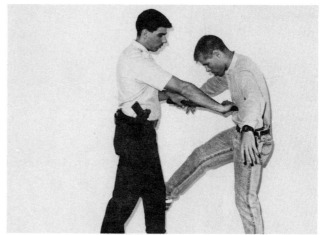

3. Counter with a butt strike to the body.

1. As his kick comes out, pick it up with your forearm and....

2. Lean back and counter with your own side-kick to his groin. This is particularly devastating because he cannot see your counter-kick until he's off-balance and your kick is connecting.

# Roundhouse Kick

1.  Use a two-handed deflection block....

2.  Then take out the other leg.

1.  Step in to jam his kick with your forearms and...

2.  Low side-kick his other knee before he can regain his balance.

46

# Push to Chest

## STICK DEFENSE:

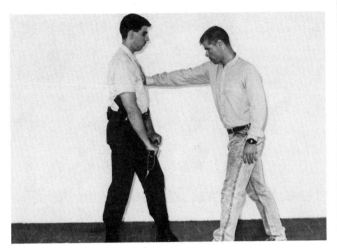

1. As he commences his pushing motion, go to a two-handed grip.

2. Slam the stick up in a rising block against the underside of his lower arm.

1. As he places his hand on you to push, clasp it to your chest as tightly as you can with both of your hands.

2. Drop back and down one step while continuing your clamp on his hand.

3. Knee kick his head out of the stadium.

# Arm or Shoulder Grab

1. As he grabs your shoulder or arm....

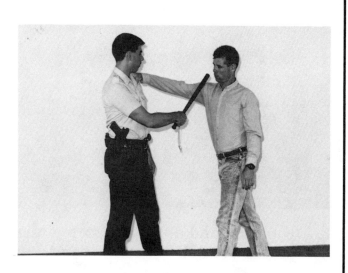

2. Slam the stick onto his deltoid (shoulder) muscle. His whole arm will temporarily lose its strength and feeling.

## UNARMED DEFENSE:

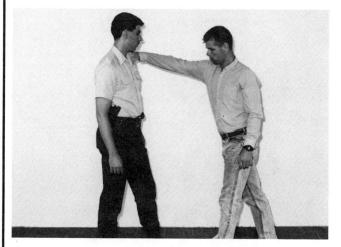

1. As he grabs your arm or shoulder...

2. Trap his holding wrist with the "V"s of your two hands.

3. Pivot and slam your armpit down on his extended elbow while you lever his hand and wrist up.

# Haymaker Punch

## STICK DEFENSE:

1. Strike his inner forearm with a two-handed block and....

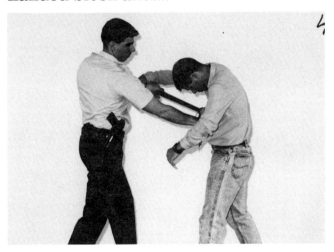

2. Strike a butt stroke into his exposed ribs.

## UNARMED DEFENSE:

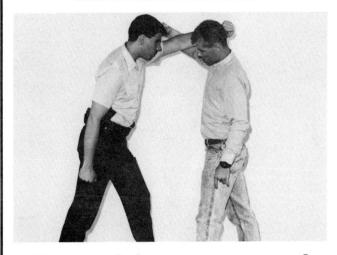

1. Step in and shoot your arm up and....

2. Around his arm so that it's trapped under your armpit while you....

3. Place your free hand on his shoulder and that your trapping arm can grab this supporting arm.

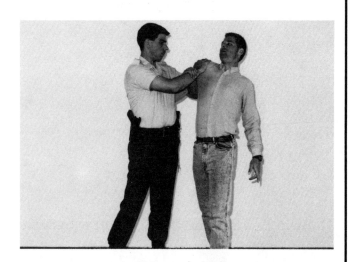

4. Lever both your wrists up to place a bind on his elbow joint. This makes a pretty good come-along.

# Boxer's Jabs

## STICK DEFENSE:

1. Don't play games with him, stay back and strike his elbows and....

1. As he jabs, use what Hapkido and Wing Chun practitioners call "Sticky Hands". Use inward-moving soft, circular blocks with your hands to absorb his force.

2. Knees.

2. As he draws back to jab again, quickly follow his retreat path with your own blow to his face.

# Tackle

### STICK DEFENSE:

1. As he goes for the tackle, bring a two-handed butt stroke....

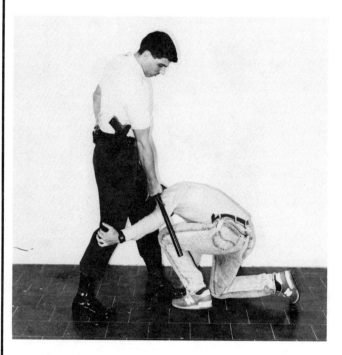

3. As he falls, strike an elbow, knee, or collarbone to finish him off.

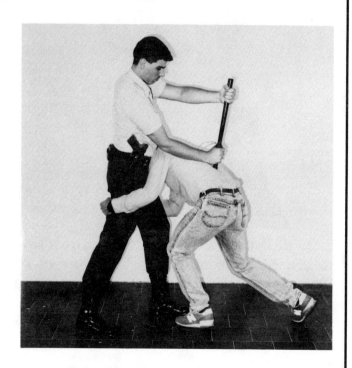

2. Down onto his back.

## UNARMED DEFENSE:

1. As he commences his tackle, execute an....

3. This drives his face into the ground while your body pins him down.

2. Atomic Elbow Drop (with your hand wide open for more power) and throw your legs out behind you.

# Front Bear-Hug

## STICK DEFENSE:

1. As he begins his hug, switch to a two-handed grip and shove the stick across his bladder area to loosen his hold and to give yourself working room.

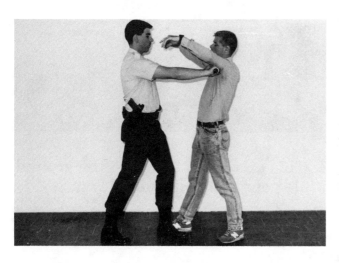

2. Keeping the same grip, explode up under his arms then....

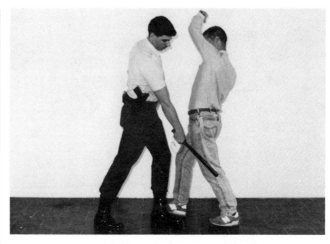

3. Take out a knee.

## UNARMED DEFENSE:

1. As he commences the hug, make your hands into fists with the tips of your thumbs protruding slightly.

2. Drive them forward into his pubic-bone region. He'll let go in a hurry.

# Rear Bear-Hug

### STICK DEFENSE:

1. As he commences the hug, bring your hands back, moving your hips slightly forward, and....

3. Strike his groin with your stick.

2. Explode your hands forward and your hips backward to release his hold then....

## UNARMED DEFENSE:

1.  As he commences the hug, bring your hands back, moving your hips slightly forward, and....

2.  Explode your hands forward and your hips backward to release his hold then....

3. Strike his groin with a backfist. I have used this in a surprise, combat situation and can vouch that it works great!

# CHAPTER 5

# DEALING WITH KNIFE ATTACKS

One of the deadlier attacks a security officer may face is the edged-weapon attack. Of course, pistols and automatic weapons at a distance greater than arm's length hold more danger; however, the stealth, speed and sheer shocking force of an assault with a bladed weapon make it particularly lethal. Many people have a deeply-rooted psychological hang-up with the idea of a blade violating their bodies.

This fear can have several effects on the potential victim ranging from paralyzing panic to berserker anger. The important things to remember are that a knife is a stabbing and slashing weapon. Of the two threats, the stab is generally more dangerous because of the high-shock-value injuries it produces which can penetrate deeply and produce severe internal damage and bleeding. The slash, on the other hand, produces disfiguring and crippling injuries that bleed profusely. For these reasons, many feel facing a knife attack is a no-win proposition.

Neutralizing the knife attack requires that it be dealt with on two different levels:

the psychological and the physical. First let's face the mental barriers. If you are cut by a knife slash in the heat of battle, the immediate pain factor will be minimal. The combination of your body's natural chemicals, adrenaline and endomorphins, will minimize pain as a survival reaction. The most you may feel at the time is a sharp stinging sensation. Of course, later on there will be more pain; however, this is true of most injuries. In addition, plastic surgery can do wonders with scars these days, so you don't have to be overly concerned in the disfiguring area. Besides, your lady or man may find such a scar lends a certain raffish look to your appearance. On the other hand, deeply penetrating stabs are very painful and can quickly render you ineffective from shock, so they are to be respected. The key aspect to keep in mind when facing a knife is that you can survive if you know what you're doing. The attitude you should take is, "Let the Bastard do his worst. I'm going to make him pay with interest!" In other words, out aggress the aggressor. Be ready to go all the way with him and make him regret he ever elected to use a knife on you.

That helps with the psychological aspects of a knife assault, now lets see what specific ways can be used to meet such an attack at the physical level. First, if you are armed with a firearm and have the time to draw, chamber a round, pull the trigger, and shoot him. Unfortunately, he may be too close or too stealthy or too quick when he initiates an attack for you to sense it in time to do that. Second, if you are not armed with a firearm and you already have your night-stick out, use it on your assailant. Lastly, if the situation leaves you no alternative but an unarmed response, you will have to use your own bodily weapons against his attack. Given this priority of choices, we will now address them in their order of preference for the more likely attacks that you may face.

# The Threats

Depending on the level of experience and motivations of your assailant, you may face any number of attack styles. If he is an inexperienced street punk, he may lead with the knife. This means he may stick the knife out in front of him in what he thinks is an intimidating manner. This is the easiest threat to neutralize in that you can see with certainty where the weapon is and it is vulnerable to counterattacks of your own. The more experienced fighter will hold his knife much further back and will hide it if he can. He will also use his free hand to attack or confuse you at the same time he launches his knife attack. You are going to have to deal with a multi-faceted attack and still be able to counter them. First, keep your eyes open at all times. Don't let him distract or redirect your attention. Keep your eyes centered on his chest and watch all other directions with your peripheral vision.

Be aware that he is going to be going all out. He won't be happy to thrust or slash once and then leave his knife out where it can be grabbed. If he can stab you once, he will try to keep on stabbing until you are down and dead (even if it takes 20 times). After all, dead people tell no tales. We will study several common attacks and effective night-stick and unarmed counters to each one that will allow you to stop him and end the struggle in your favor.

The most common attacks are:

- **The Straight Thrust**

- **The Hooking Thrust**

- **The Forehand Slash**

- **The Backhand Slash or Stab**

- **The "Ice-pick" Attack**

- **"Ninja" Slashes**

- **The Belly Rip-up**

# Stick Defense Theory

Most of the following stick defenses involve multiple hits. When you practice with padded sticks, you'll quickly discover that it is possible to use the rebound of a striking stick to set up another strike. If you use lots of wrist snap in your strikes, it's possible to make firm contacts to targets three or four times in one second. It's important to realize that for each target you strike, several more will suddenly appear. Never stop with just one hit in practice. Learn to think in terms of multiples so that you can keep the pressure on him. This will insure that he never regains the initiative.

# The Theory of Un-armed Knife Defense

We will use a standardized approach to countering any kind of knife attack. It consists of three elements:

- **Block the attack.**

- **Control the weapon.**

- **Counter-attack.**

Regardless of the threat, we must first neutralize the initial threat or we won't live long enough worry about the other aspects of defense. In each of the following series of techniques, we will always strive to block the attack in the safest, most effective manner possible. Then we will seek to control the assailant's use of his weapon so that we will have a chance to render him combat-ineffective with a counter-attack before he can deliver another attack.

# Straight Thrust Counters

Our assailant may use a straight thrust to stab deeply into the guard's body cavity. Attacks don't come any more direct than this. He will be thrusting as strongly and as quickly as he can. He will not leave the knife out there in front for you to grab his arm or hand. Your only chance will be to make solid contact with his arm as it is coming in, jarring it enough to stop it and allowing you to then control and counter it. You will also have to deal with his free hand at the same time.

### STICK DEFENSE:

**2. Use the rebound effect to lay the stick alongside his neck.**

**1. Step back and snap the nightstick down hard on his inner wrist. This will block the thrust and numb his hand so that he can't hold the knife any longer.**

**3. Then go for his legs to weaken them.**

**UNARMED DEFENSE:**

1. Slam your wrist bones into the assailant's inner wrist tendons. This blocks the thrust and weakens his grip.

2. Immediately grab his hand with your opposite-side hand and....

3. Re-enforce your grip and turn his wrist over into a wrist-lock and pull sharply.

# Hooking Thrust Counters

## STICK DEFENSE:

1. Use a two-handed striking block to stop the thrust.

2. Step back and counterstrike onto his hand to knock his knife loose.

1. This is one of the tougher threats to defend against since there's so little margin for error. This may be further complicated by his use of his free hand as a distractor or secondary attack. In this case, block both his hands outward and....

2. Try to kick his testicles up to his throat to slow him down and to take his mind off any further knife attacks.

3.  Then go for a wrist-lock disarm.

# Forehand Slash Counters

## STICK DEFENSE:

1.  Strike his inner wrist and ....

2. Rebound around and down to the side of his knee.

## UNARMED DEFENSE:

1.  Step in and execute a scissors block to....

2.  Shatter his elbow.

# Backhand Slash Counters

## STICK DEFENSE:

1. Snap a backhanded strike into his elbow to block and disable his knife arm.

2. Rebound around, snapping a strike into his short ribs.

1. Step in and jam his arm with your forearms.

2. Grab his wrist and pivot while pulling his arm straight.

3. Execute an elbow shatter.

# Backhand Stab Counters

### STICK DEFENSE:

Treat the same as you would for a backhand slash.

### UNARMED DEFENSE:

This is more difficult to defend against than the slash since the leading knife point and blade make it difficult to grab the wrist.

1. Step in to jam and....

2. Execute a knee kick into his midsection while controlling his knife arm.

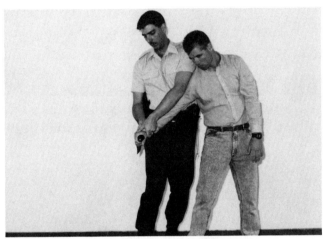

3. Then go for a wrist-crank on his knife hand by grabbing the base of his thumb then....

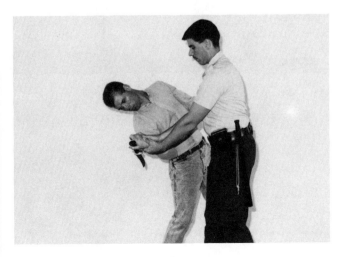

4.  Re-enforcing your grip with two hands and levering around and down.

# "Ice-Pick" Attacks

1. Two-hand block the descending knife arm up and in.

3. A knee strike.

**UNARMED DEFENSE:**

1.   Lunge forward and block the descending arm and bring your free hand up behind the knife hand to....

2.   Lock up his arm and bend it backwards while you....

3. Continue to move forward.  I saw this technique used in a street situation once and the assailant's knife flew about 35 feet behind him.

# "Ninja" Slashes

## STICK DEFENSE:

1. Although many martial art instructors teach this style of knife fighting, it is an inferior method. They seem to think that since a knife can't be seen easily, everyone is fooled. What a laugh! If you know where his hand and arm are, you know where the knife is.

2. Defend as you would against slashes or hooking thrusts.

## UNARMED DEFENSE:

Defend as you would against....

1. Forehand slashes or....

2. Backhand stabs

# Belly Rip-Out

1.  This is a vertical circular thrust up into the belly.  It's similar to an upper-cut in boxing.  Deflect it inward with a two-handed block and....

2.  Start striking at elbows and other targets of opportunity.

1.  Deflect with your forearm and....

2.  Execute a low side-kick to break/dislocate his knee.

# CHAPTER 6

# DEALING WITH CLUB ATTACKS

There are two possibilities when you may need to know how to defend against a club. Both presume you're not carrying a sidearm or that there isn't time to employ it. The first case is when the assailant brings a club of some sort with him. The second is if he scuffles with you and somehow manages to take your nightstick away. In either case, you are now facing a potentially lethal weapon that has the capability to severely damage or kill you. We will consider the following threat scenarios:

- **Forehand swings**

- **Overhead swings**

- **Backhand swings**

- **Baseball Bat swings**

- **Pokes**

In each case, we will present a nightstick counter and an unarmed counter. Although there are many such techniques, we will only illustrate a few to keep down the confusion factor.

# Forehand Swings

### STICK DEFENSE

### UNARMED DEFENSE:

1. Squat and counterstrike his inner wrist (remember to use a lot of wrist-snap in your strike). The squat will bring your head low enough to be out of danger when his numbed hand releases his club in mid-swing. It also positions you nicely for....

1. Step inside his swing, using a scissors block with both your forearms to....

2. A follow-on strike to the nerve point on the outside of his knee, which can be followed by any number of other strikes to vulnerable targets as his leg collapses.

2. Shatter his elbow.

# Overhead Swings

### STICK DEFENSE:

1. Step 45 degrees outside and forward while executing a snappy backhand counterstrike to the outside of his wrist.

2. Use the rebound off his wrist to start the motion for....

3. A circular strike to the back of his knee or his Achilles tendon.

**UNARMED DEFENSE:**

1. Lunge 45 degrees forward, shooting your arm forward and upward to....

2. Encircle his arm and neck while your shoulder drives into the nerve center in his armpit.

3. Lock your hands tightly and squeeze while....

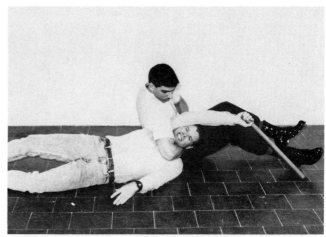

4. Continuing to lunge forward to bulldog him down. This technique produces incredible pain. When you practice this, do it slowly because it is possible to break the assailant's neck when done violently.

# Backhand Swings

1. Gripping the stick at both ends, snap a blocking counterstrike into his wrist while lunging to meet his attack.

2. Snap a strike to his rear knee and....

3. Step behind him to snap another strike into his other knee.

75

**UNARMED DEFENSE:**

1. Lunge in and jam his arms with your forearms.

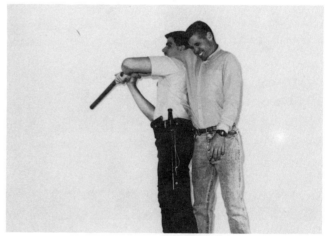

3. Snap his elbow over your shoulder.

2. Grab his club-hand and pivot so you can....

# Baseball Bat Swings

## STICK DEFENSE

1. Don't try to meet his heavier club directly. Your's would be shattered. Instead, use a two-handed block against his arms, then....

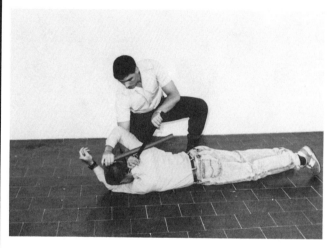

3. Pivot and drag him forward and down so that he eats dirt.

2. Hook your stick's end behind his neck.

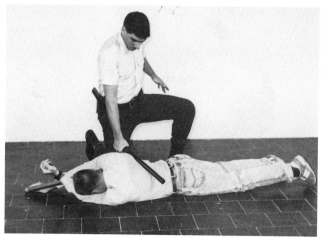

4. Follow up with strikes to nerve or muscle points on his arms so that he can't use them to swing the bat anymore.

**UNARMED DEFENSE:**

1. Timing is everything here. DO NOT ATTEMPT TO BLOCK A BAT! IT'S A GOOD WAY TO GET BROKEN ARMS OR RIBS! As he swings, ....

2. Pull back to let it pass by harmlessly.

3. As it passes your body, explode forward to....

4. Bury the point of your shoulder into his ribs with a flying tackle and put him down as hard as you can. Keep hitting and kicking until he doesn't feel like getting up anymore.

# Pokes

1. Use a two-handed deflecting block and counter with a....

2. Butt strike into his solar plexus. Follow up with more strikes to vulnerable points as required.

### UNARMED DEFENSE:

1. Deflect the poke with....

2. A forearm and immediately rotate the same forearm to a horizontal position to follow up with an....

3. Elbow strike to his face or throat.

80

# CHAPTER 7

# PISTOL DISARMING

The one point heard over and over in security guard pistol classes is, "Don't stand too close to an assailant with a drawn weapon. He might take it away from you." What you'll seldom hear; however, is **how** it might be taken away. This chapter is designed to provide you with the necessary knowledge to take away an assailant's gun if he gets too close to you. **These techniques should never be attempted if the assailant is not standing within arm's length of you!**

## Your Advantage

You have one advantage over your assailant— you know when you're going to move, but he doesn't. This allows you to take advantage of his reaction lag-time. A good illustration of this point is a person who has to bring his car to a panic-stop. His reaction-lag time is based upon the following: First, he must see a danger somewhere out in front of the car. Second, he must recognize it as a threat. Third, he must lift his foot off the accelerator. Fourth, he must step on the brakes.

The same is true for your assailant. First, he must see your movement. Second, he must perceive it as a threat. Third, he must squeeze the trigger while tracking a target.

In both instances, it takes a finite time for a person to react to a threat. Your advantage is you know when you're going to move and your assailant doesn't. Once you commence your take-away technique, your assailant must go through the reaction lag-time sequence. **Your attempt must be faster than that lag! For this reason, it is imperative that once you start a technique, you must be totally committed to it. Do not hesitate once you have started. If you do, you will eat a bullet the hard way.**

## Key points

Similar to knife defenses, pistol take-aways require that you block / touch the limb or hand holding the weapon; control the weapon; counter or take away the weapon.

We will address the following threat situations:

- **Single-hand grip to our front**

- **Double-hand grip to our front**

- **Single-hand grip assassination foil from the side**

- **Double-hand grip assassination foil from the side**

- **Gun to the head from the rear**

- **Gun to the mid-level back from the rear**

- **Gun to the lower spine from the rear**

- **Hand gripping collar with gun pointed into back**

- **Rear bar-arm choke with gun pointed at the head**

# Take-aways to the Front

SINGLE HAND GRIP:

1. If he sticks his pistol out in front and says, "Hands up!"

3. It's stripped out of his hand.

2. Pull his gun wrist toward you (immediately pulling his gun out of alignment with your body) and push the weapon forward with your other hand until...

4. If the round didn't go off into his body, use the gun as a club. This is considered the surest counter since you don't know if the gun is loaded or not.

## DOUBLE HAND GRIP:

1. If he sticks the gun out in front in a double-handed grip, bring both of your hands up under his gun.

2. Shove his weapon up as you squat down a little and...

3. Rotate the weapon back into him. If the gun is cocked, the pressure on his finger will cause it to fire somewhere between straight overhead and straight back at him. His finger inside the trigger guard will commence to dislocate or break at this point.

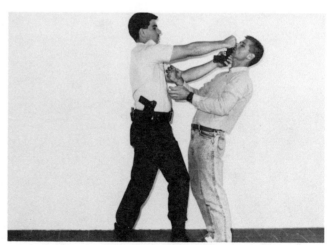

4. Strip the gun out of his hands by pulling straight back toward yourself and stepping back simultaneously. If he's still standing, club him down.

# Take-Aways to the Side

These next two techniques are suited for situations where a gunman attempts to shoot someone to his front when there is a security officer to his side.

SINGLE-HANDED GRIP
ASSASSINATION FOIL:

1. Begin a scissors movement with your near-side hand above his arm and your gun-side hand below his weapon.

2. Drive your hand down onto his wrist while you slap/catch the gun up and...

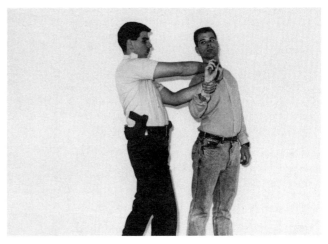

3. Rotate it back toward him (thereby minimizing the danger to innocent people in the immediate area).

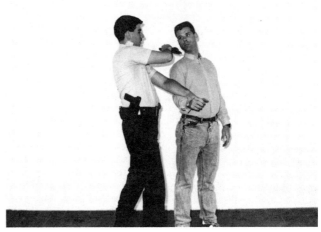

4. Strip it out of his hand

## DOUBLE-HANDED GRIP
## ASSASSINATION FOIL:

1. Drive your near-side arm down onto the crooks of his elbows while slap/ catching his weapon up and...

3. Strip it away.

2. Rotate it up and back.

# Take-Aways to the Rear

These should only be attempted if the gun is touching you so you know exactly where it is! If the weapon isn't touching you, don't try anything! Notice how many of the following techniques are the same basic moves with adjustments made for the different heights of the pistol's placement. This simplifies training and increases your chances for success.

**GUN TO THE HEAD / OUTSIDE LINE:**

1. From the starting position with your hands in the air....

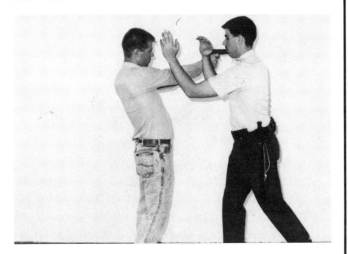

2. Pivot in place to touch your forearms to his arm.

3. Grip his gun hand in a mutually-supported double-hand grip (similar to the grip used in the wrist lock come-along).

4. Execute what is known as a wrist crank by powering his hand up, around, and down till he drops the weapon.

## GUN TO THE HEAD / INSIDE LINE:

1. Pivot, maintaining arm contact.

2. Reach under and grab the gun barrel.

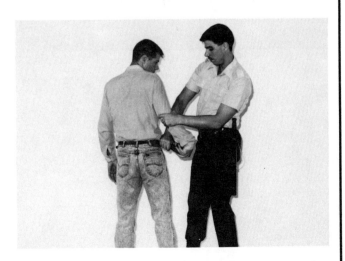

3. Rotate the gun down and out to strip it out of his hand.

## GUN TO MID-LEVEL / OUTSIDE LINE:

1. Pivot and use your forearms to maintain contact with his gunarm.

2. Grab and....

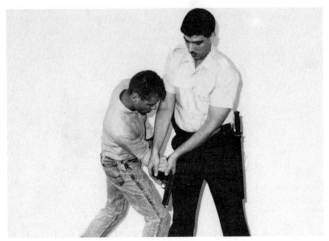

3. Wrist crank.

## GUN TO MID-LEVEL / INSIDE LINE

1. Pivot and touch with forearms.

2. Grab his hand in a wrist-lock grip and....

3. Execute the wrist-lock, forcing the hand and gun back into him until he drops it. With disarming wrist-lock and wrist-crank techniques, it is best to execute them violently with a lot of body English. Don't cut him any slack!

## GUN TO LOW-LEVEL / OUTSIDE LINE

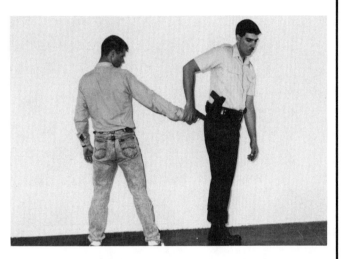

1. Simultaneously rise up on your toes, bring the "V" of your hand and thumb from up to down upon the receiver group of the weapon and....

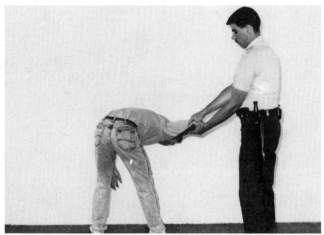

3. Get the double-handed grip on his gun and hand and....

2. Shove it down and pivot.

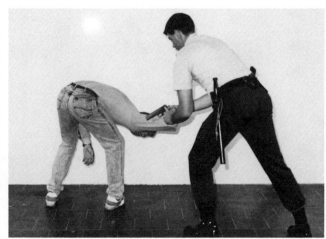

4. Execute a wrist-lock.

## GUN TO LOW LEVEL / INSIDE LINE:

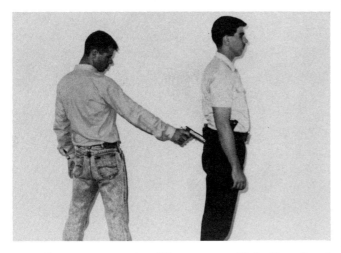

1.  Start exactly like you did the last lowline technique.

3.  Execute a wrist-crank.

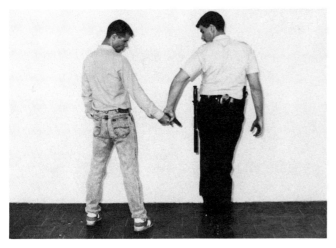

2.  Shove down, pivot, and grip.

## BAR ARM CHOKE / GUN TO HEAD:

1. This is a classic hostage / body shield situation. As he pulls you backward, pretend to go faint from fear, forcing him to support more of your weight. This also takes his attention off you as a threat and allows you to shift into a better position.

3. Immediately rotate the gun back, around, and down....

2. Quickly bring up your opposite hand until it can grab the gun barrel. DO NOT USE THE SAME-SIDE HAND BECAUSE HE WILL BE ABLE TO FEEL AND SEE IT MOVE BEFORE IT CAN GET INTO POSITION!

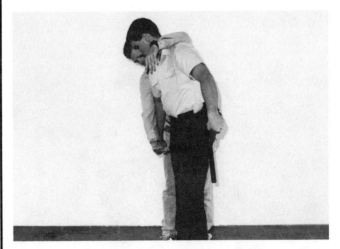

4. Which will strip the weapon out of his hand.

# CHAPTER 8

# GROUND FIGHTING

It's been said that about 80% of street fights end up on the ground. The possibility of this scenario cannot be ignored, so we've included some basics. It doesn't matter how good a fighter you might be, you can never know when a combination of circumstances might dump you on the ground. If this happens to you, don't panic. You can still fight effectively from the ground.

These techniques are also useful for fighting on ice, steep hillsides, or other uncertain footing conditions.

# Defending to the Front

1. **Get on your side and hip. Place your hands on the ground and raise your head up so you can see what's going on. Keep your bottom leg on the ground and raise your other leg.**

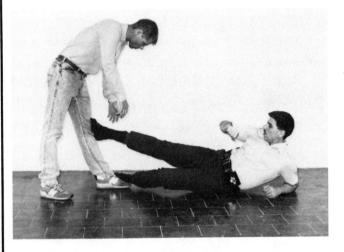

3. **Stomp into the side of his knee to put him down and get up.**

2. **As your assailant moves in, hook your bottom foot behind his heel and...**

# Defending to the Side

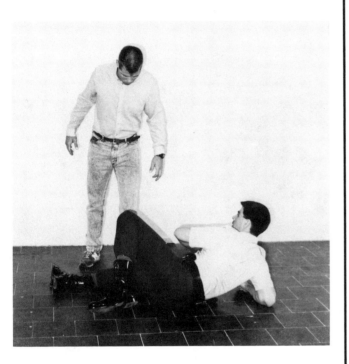

1. As your assailant attacks from the side, chamber back your upper knee and...

2. Kick into his groin with your pointed toes. Get up.

# Defending Against A Stomp

# Defending Against a Body Straddle

1. As the assailant raises his foot to stomp, catch his foot with your hands before it gains too much downward momentum and...

1. Buck up with your hips while you push against his arms toward the direction of least resistance. Get up.

2. Twist his foot sharply to dump him on the ground then get up.

2. Push your thumb into pressure points, grab and squeeze his scrotum, bite, do whatever it takes to get away from his control and get up!

# CHAPTER 9

# TRAINING AIDS AND DRILLS

## Suggestions for the Trainer

You may find the following information useful when designing a training program for your police or security force.

**Training Time and Schedules:** Rather than subject your students to an all-day, day-after-day training program, it is better to train them no more than two hours at a time, once or twice a week, until they have mastered all the techniques. It is better to have learned a few techniques really well than to have learned them all superficially. Training sessions of longer than two hours risk injuries and inattention due to fatigue. Start every class with a quick review of the previous class's material. Hold periodic practical exams to force the students to review all previous material.

**Realism in Training:** The more realistic you can make your training program, the better chance your people will have on the street. For example, use the actual night-stick to become accustomed to its weight and feel and use the light-weight, padded version mentioned later in this chapter so the students can learn to counter and execute techniques at full speed to gain the appropriate reflexes. De-emphasize sports training that turns training sessions into contests with points and fair and foul targets. Train to develop street reflexes in an environment that recognizes no rules. The only rule your classes should worry about is The Golden Rule, which demands self-control out of necessity. Once some degree of self-control has been acquired in unarmed fighting, the students should don full protective pads and pick up the training tempo.

**Combat Pistol Shoot:** Professor Ray Wood, a fellow Hapkido teacher and director of the hand-to-hand training program at the U.S. Military Academy, West Point, New York, has developed a hand-to-hand equivalent of a combat pistol shoot. His cadet students are required to pass through as many as twenty testing stations. At each station a different situational scenario has been established. Each situation consists of role player(s) and a lane grader. The students are given a brief situational description and are required to demonstrate an ability to use appropriate force, to use good technique, and to show aggressiveness.

My favorite station is where the student walks into the room and sees one role player sitting on the floor and another up against the wall in the search position. The lane grader tells the student that the role player on the floor is a peaceful demonstrator and that the student's mission is to transport the peaceful demonstrator up against the wall. Naturally the appropriate response would be for the student to put a come-along on the role player and take him over against the wall. What the lane grader hasn't said is the role player against the wall is a violent demonstrator. As soon as the student turns his back on the violent one, he gets nailed and has to fight his way out. The object lesson is that he should never take too much for granted.

# Training Aids

**Picture 1** shows both a rubber knife and a wooden training knife. The rubber knife is great for realism in photos; however, it's too forgiving for realistic training purposes. We prefer to use the wooden version in our training classes because it will punish a student if he makes a mistake. No one gets

seriously injured; however, a good bruise serves as an excellent reminder to execute a counter properly the next time. Pain makes a wonderful incentive.

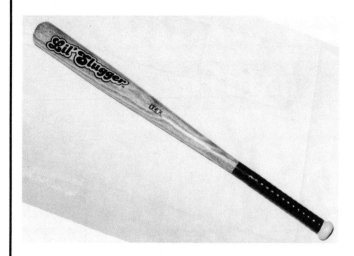

**Picture 2** shows a whiffle-ball bat. These make wonderful club training aids. They are light enough to use at speed without causing serious damage to the students.

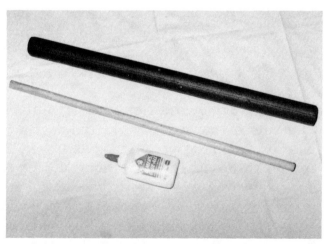

**Picture 3** shows how an excellent padded training nightstick can be made out of a light-weight pine dowel rod, some pipe insulation, and some white wood glue.

Picture 4 shows a rubber gun alongside a .45 automatic. The rubber gun is cheap (available from many martial art supply houses advertised in martial arts magazines) and is relatively safe. The actual pistol is good to teach how to apply leverage properly (it doesn't bend) and it can be dry-fired to demonstrate that a takeaway technique really works. **One word of caution, it's really easy to break an aggressor's finger if he leaves it inside the trigger housing during the execution of the takeaway. Be careful!**

# Training Drills

Here are a number of training drills and concepts that have proven invaluable in our training workshops.

**Slo-Mo Talk Thru's:** To gain proficiency at fighting, you have to fight; however, no one ever said you'll learn everything there is to know by going full-force from day one. That invites injuries and bad habits. What works really well is to talk through the fight scenario first and as it develops, while executing attacks and counter-attacks in slow-motion. As skills increase, so should the speed until they are able to go full speed. This method allows the participants to see and understand the logic-train of the various moves. It won't be long until they have grasped the assigned lesson and are inventing effective

techniques of their own.

**Stick Quick-Draws:** Quick-drawing the night stick with either hand and executing blocks, strikes, and pokes into a target are absolutely essential to hone automatic reflexes for the street. You'll find this carries over onto the job when the students start walking their patrols while they unconsciously keep their hand on or near the stick handle at all times. These are good survival instincts and may save a few lives.

**Poke the Spot:** To develop accuracy with the stick, stand close to a wall, pick a spot and try to poke it. Do it over and over until you're hitting it with regularity. Then, find another spot at a different height. Once you've developed accuracy with one angle of poke, try another angle or a different hand.

**Up-Against-the-Wall Fighting Drills**: The defenders start out with their backs to the wall or in a corner. The attackers seek to capitalize on their plight while the defenders seek to use these obstacles to their own advantage.

**Back-to-Backs:** These are great to teach the realities of grappling on the ground. The only rules are to control techniques for safety's sake and each fighter must stay on the ground, no higher than his knees. The drill begins with the two protagonists sitting back-to-back on a wrestling or tumbling mat. The signal to start is given and they turn toward each other and fight like mad. The contest is over when the instructor says stop or when one fighter gives up. Since about 80% of street fights end up on the ground, this drill is absolutely essential.

# Conclusion

Although these drills and aids have proven helpful, they are by no means the final word in training techniques. I'm sure you can think up lots of ones on your own that replicate realistic street requirements. If it makes sense and it works, go for it. If you find some that work well for you, we'd sure like to hear about them through our publishing and consulting address in the back section of this manual.

# CHAPTER 10

# UNIVERSAL FORCE DYNAMICS

## Background

Back in 1981, I began thinking about all the self defense students I had trained and who the best ones had been. Oddly enough, all of my premier students had been Intelligence analysts like myself. Smugly I thought, "That's because they were smart guys." When I took the time to really study it, I realized natural intelligence wasn't the only reason these students had progressed so rapidly and so well. I had been fortunate to teach lots of smart people. What made these Intelligence analysts so different? Then in a blinding flash of the obvious, it finally struck home. The differentiating factor wasn't natural intelligence, rather it was in how their intelligence was used in day-to-day experiences.

Intelligence analysts live for the rank smell of conflict. Every day they deal with enemy capabilities, enemy intentions, and how these all can be orchestrated to bring down agony and defeat upon the good guys. In other words, they are major players in the management of conflict.

When they got out on the mats with my class, they brought with them a mind-set already keyed to strife and conflict. True, they were accustomed to dealing with great armies and grand strategies; however, they saw individual combat with the same eyes. When a movement was explained, they could picture it in their head as something equivalent to a movement on a battlefield. Because of this familiarity with conflict, the tactics and strategy of personal, one-on-one fighting was obvious to them. They were able to bypass hours of painful practice to gain an instinctive understanding of the essence of the martial arts. Because they understood the reasons for movements from the very beginning, they were able to focus their concentration on the physical rudiments and apply them correctly much sooner than others were capable of doing.

I thought to myself, "If this idea of understanding conflict management can work from the top down, why shouldn't it work from the bottom up?" The only problem of implementing that approach lay in the seemingly complex field of the martial arts. There are over a thousand different styles or "Ways". Like many religious sects, each Master was saying, "Lo, here is the Way, the only Way." I set out to study what was similar and what was different about each of these different styles. In reviewing many books, in talking with many practitioners, and in considering several of the styles with which I had personal experience, I came to realize that there were certain universal principles with which one could respond to force, any force. These principles were present in all the arts. What made the arts different from one another was the manner in which the principles were applied to each style.

What began as a philosophical exercise soon became an obsession. I couldn't help but analyze many daily-life situations all around me. I discovered these principles were not only universal to the martial arts, they were universal to all conflicts: business and sales situations, leadership and management, military tactics and strategy, politics, government policy making, and even interpersonal relationships.

To help you better understand the nature of conflict on the street, I am including this chapter on Universal Force Dynamics to give you a language for personal combat. As a bonus, I will also describe a few day-to-day parallels so you can use this concept in your daily lives.

# Components

**Universal Force Dynamics** (UFD) consists of six principles and twenty-two dynamic factors. The principles are the operating laws and the factors and are influencing agents. The factors equate (but are more inclusive) to the principles of war. These principles and factors can be combined in more ways than most people can count (ap-

proximately $3 \times 10^{29}$). That fact alone is what makes strategy and human relations so blessedly complex. The principles and factors are rarely, if ever, used alone, by themselves. They may be used one after another or several together simultaneously.

# Purpose

For the security officer or policeman, there are four goals which UFD will assist you in dealing with an assailant:

- **To deny him opportunities**

- **To degrade his fighting techniques and defenses**

- **To disrupt his attacks**

- **To arrest and control him until help arrives**

## UFD Principles

## Principle 1: Avoiding Force

This pertains to mobility in battle. It means staying out of range or moving aside to let a kick, blow, or thrust pass by. It also means ducking under a punch or jumping over a trip. In life it means choosing not to argue about a touchy subject or choosing not to compete in a certain market.

The defender moves to the side, away from a thrust.

# Principle 2: Leading Force

Causing an opponent's attack to extend or travel further than he intended it to go. This will throw him off balance, after which the defender can take control. We see this in the courtroom when a lawyer asks a leading question to trick a witness into saying more than he intended.

1.   The defender grabs an attacker's punch.

2.   He pulls the punching arm further than it was intended to travel, bringing the attacker off balance.

3.   He then takes control by putting the assailant in a carotid lock-up.

# Principle 3: Turning Force

Change the direction of a kick or blow, thereby taking it off the target line. It will change a straight-line attack into a portion of or a complete circle. It will cause a circular attack to travel in a different circle. In the same manner, we may change the direction of a conversation if it seems safer to do so.

**A straight-line kick is redirected by a deflection block.**

# Principle 4: Absorbing Force

Absorb your opponent's force until it is rendered harmless or has been exhausted. Muhammad Ali used force absorption perfectly. Whenever he faced an opponent who was known to be a strong slugger, he would cover his face and body and lay back on the ring ropes. His attacker's blows would be transmitted through Ali's arms, through his body, and into the resilient ring ropes which acted as shock absorbers. When the opponent got too tired to keep up his guard, Ali would pick him apart. We absorb force whenever we let words fall on deaf ears or if we're unresponsive.

**"Sticky Hands" is an ideal force absorbtion technique.**

# Principle 5: Force Against Force

Two forces come together to the detriment of one. This means blowing through another's defenses or hard-blocking an incoming attack. It overpowers an opponent through the superior use of strength. It's also blowing through a football line or shouting down someone else in an argument.

**Using the superior power of a nightstick to overpower a choker.**

# Principle 6: Force Harmonization

It is possible to use an opponent's force as your own. You can also add your force to an opponent's to speed his up or to lead it further than he intended. Policemen answering domestic squabble calls often see one aspect of this principle when the beaten wife starts fighting the policemen as they take her husband out the door. Here, two antagonists are joining together against an outside party. Harmonization is not unusual in sales situations. A customer's adamant objection may be turned into a benefit that clenches the sale by a salesman who knows how to manipulate peoples' points of view.

**1. The defender grabs a punch.**

**2. He uses the attacker's momentum.**

**3. And throws him to the ground.**

As mentioned before, these principles are normally used in combinations. For example, you can avoid force by sidestepping a punch, lead and harmonize by pulling the punch as it goes by, turning it into a throw, harmonizing with the assailant's momentum. When the attacker lands, he may use force absorption by executing a break-fall while you might use force against force to put him away with a powerful blow. Every single fight scenario can be described in these terms.

Now that we see how the principles are involved in conflict, let's expand our picture to include the dynamic factors and see how they influence fights and conflicts.

# Dynamic Factors

## Factor 1: Balance

This signifies both physical and emotional balance. The idea is to maintain yours while disrupting an assailant's. You can't move effectively if you're off balance. Neither can you fight effectively if fear and anger cause you to lose control and concentration. You must maintain your physical and emotional equilibrium. This is true in day-to-day life as well.

# Factor 2: Battle-Awareness

You must stay in touch with what's going on in the fight. You should be aware of what an opponent is doing; what is happening to your front, rear, sides, and above and below you; what the terrain is like, and whether there are any obstacles that can be used. You need to use all six senses: sight, sound, touch, smell, taste, and psi. These senses must be extended equally in all directions. Some martial artists call this "soft eyes". When facing an assailant, you should center your eyes on his chest. All his limb and body movements are telegraphed through this area and all his limbs lie within your peripheral vision. If you watch only his eyes, feet, face, or hands, he might feint with one them and follow up from a direction that you aren't watching.

We do the same thing in business when we conduct market surveys to determine the nature of our area of competition.

# Factor 3: Cohesiveness

It helps to stick to a game plan or a fighting strategy as long as it works. Techniques and movements should support one another. For instance, if you should block a punch, the end of the blocking movement should automatically set up the start of a counterattack, which in turn sets up an opportunity to finish off your opponent. In other words, your fighting style should flow logically, just as your argument should flow logically if you want to win it.

# Factor 4: Concentration of Power / Resources

Bringing your physical and mental attention to bear on a target involves concentrating all your force on a single point in time. Martial artists call this the "one point" or "moment". Perform a kick or strike so the weapon travels at a relaxed pace until it explodes into the target with maximum force. This is called "snap power" and is similar to snapping a wet towel at someone in the locker room. The towel travels deceptively slow until the very tip of it snaps around, delivering a stinging crack at the target.

Another rule of thumb related to force concentration is to attack wide, area-targets with small, narrow weapons. If you were to slap an opponent's stomach with an open hand, it would probably leave no more damage than a stinging sensation. However, if you used the ends of your stiffened fingers or a nightstick butt, your opponent would be bothered much more.

Likewise, if you focus your attention and energies on one problem in your life at a time, you will be more likely to be successful than if you try to solve all of them at the same time.

# Factor 5: Conservation of Power/Resources

You should always conserve your energy, save a little in reserve in case a supreme effort is suddenly needed. Two essential aspects are inner calmness and a degree of self-awareness. Experienced martial artists learn to use economical movements. Often an experienced fighter in his 30s or 40s can hold his own against much younger, stronger opponents because of this factor. The older fighter must learn to garner his energy by seeking to economize his motions, and to control the situation. If the younger fighter is constantly having to react, he will eventually run out of steam. The older fighter will then have the advantage.

If you constantly rush full-speed through life without taking a break now and then, you will run out of steam. Learn to garner your energy in life as well.

# Factor 6: Coordination

Not only is coordination essential in the physical or athletic sense, your body and mind have to work together as one. If you attempt to use a fighting technique while you are thinking that you probably won't be successful, there are better-than-even odds that you will fail because you have not committed yourself to action. Indecisiveness destroys an attack's or a defense's coordination and effectiveness. Remember, to harmonize with one's force, you must first be coordinated.

Coordination is important in life as well. Think of all the attention paid to color coordination or to a well coordinated sales campaign.

# Factor 7: Deception

We seek to deceive our enemies by hiding our weak and strong areas and by masking our intentions. We do this by pretending to be weaker or stronger than we actually are so that we can elicit a response or attitude from our enemy. The use of feints or fakes with our head, feet, legs, hands, or body exists primarily to deceive the enemy.

Deception is used all the time in our lives. The most dangerous kind is that which we do to ourselves.

# Factor 8: Distance

This factor deals primarily with the range between opponents. The expression, "keeping your distance," means to stay at a range where you can effectively counter or attack your opponent while maintaining your own safety. In a personal combat situation, there are three ranges:

• **Long Range- only long-range weapons such as kicks or leaping strikes are dangerous threats.**

• **Midrange- This is the maximum danger area because most weapons and defenses are within reach of one another.**

• **Close Range- If you have a shorter reach than your opponent, this is the safest place other than being totally out of his reach. Once you get inside his long or midrange weapons / defenses, you can use interior or close-range weapons such as head butts, elbow strikes, forearms, knees, and chokes to great effect!**

One of the better examples in life is the amount of emotional distance one keeps between himself and other people.

# Factor 9: Effort

This refers to the amount of power or speed you put into your techniques. In life, it's how much of ourselves which we put into it.

# Factor 10: Initiative

It helps to get the drop on an opponent.

As an old boxer once said, "Whoever gets there firstest with the mostest wins." This also means to rely on your own inventiveness or judgement in absence of instructions or orders. It is also the willingness to take a risk.

The equivalent in life is being willing to take a calculated risk before anyone else.

# Factor 11: Maneuver

This is the act of moving from one point to another. The object of this mobility is to catch your opponent in a disadvantageous position. You may attempt to get your opponent off balance to gain time to maneuver to a more advantageous position.

In life we need to be flexible, to try different solutions and be able to quickly move on to another solution if that one didn't work.

# Factor 12: Momentum

This factor is neutral in nature in that it can work both for and against you. Momentum is the moving inertia of maneuver. You can use momentum to maintain the initiative; however, your momentum can be used against you if you allow your opponent to harmonize with <u>your</u> force.

Momentum is the foundation of routine in our lives. Once we start doing things a certain way, it's easier to continue doing them that way rather than to change.

# Factor 13: Position

This is the placement of your body in relationship to your assailant's.

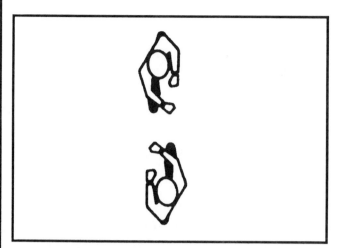

**Frontal positions**

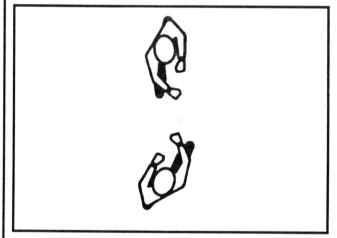

**Inside positions**

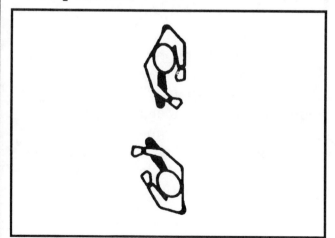

**Outside positions**

108

Being out of position means to be at an ineffective, weak, or dangerous location. A bad position in life means that your life circumstances are not good, i.e. "I'm not in the position to buy that just yet."

# Factor 14: Security

You must strive to keep yourself protected prior to and during a fight. If you kick, remember to position your blocking hands and arms where they can provide protection from a counterattack. Do not communicate your intentions.

Security, or safety, is one of the primary psychological motivators in our lives.

# Factor 15: Self-Awareness

This is the ability to monitor, observe, and understand where we are in the battle (or in life) and our relationship to our situation or environment. This goes hand-in-hand with Battle-Awareness.

# Factor 16: Situation

How we react to a threat depends on the environment, the attacker, and ourselves. For example, if a good friend at a party gets drunk and wild and attempts to choke you, you'll want to control and contain his violence without hurting either one of you. On the other hand, if a mugger on the street tries to choke you, you'll probably want to waste him. The same threat, a choke, in both cases; however, very different situations tailored your response. Our situation colors everything we do in life.

# Factor 17: Surprise

The unexpected disturbs an opponent's concentration and timing. For instance, if you spit or flick a cigarette into an attacker's eyes and immediately follow up with a punch to his face, he will not likely see the threat and may not be able to block it. An old saying says, "Nobody likes surprises." This is true in everything we do. Always strive to be the surpriser and not the surprisee.

# Factor 18: Tempo

This is how slow or fast you move. Quickness is always a positive factor in a fight; however, sometimes a change of pace can disrupt an opponent. The tempo of our lives determines how much we accomplish and how much energy we expend.

# Factor 19: Thinking / Acting Through the Objective

Never apply a blow exactly where the target is. Always aim for a point somewhere behind it. When you strike at a target, your subconscious mind tells you to start slowing the blow before contact is made out of fear the fist might get hurt. This slows the blow and, paradoxically, actually increases the probability of self injury because the fist relaxes slightly. If we think through a target, the blow is delivered at full force with a tight fist. Likewise, is we think beyond our first blow to our second, third, and fourth blows as well, we are able to keep constant pressure on our assailant and increase our chances of winning. It's like a chess game where you always want to think several moves ahead.

This factor, used day-to-day, is the essence of goal setting.

# Factor 20: Timing

Timing is a critical element to success in any endeavor, fighting or otherwise. For example, if someone throws a punch at you and you are late getting your block into place, you will be struck. The same is true if you are too early and allow the block to pass by the area needing protection. Similarly, the child who asks a parent for permission to do some activity is less likely to get it if that parent is tired and harried. It's better to wait for the right moment.

# Factor 21: Vector

This is the direction in which a force travels. It is three-dimensional. Picture yourself in the center of a sphere, as opposed to a circle, and relate to angles to or from the center of that sphere. In life, this can be where someone's coming from, a point of view.

# Factor 22: Weapon / Force Selection

The options are endless. Many books have been written detailing the parts of the body that can be used as weapons, not to mention the many specialized and field-expedient weapons. The important point to remember is that weapon and force selection are driven by the situation and your capabilities, preferences, and opportunities. For example, if you already have the nightstick out, use it. If you don't have it ready, the choice of bare hands or stick depends on how much time there is and the degree of threat.

This equates to strategy or option selection in real life.

# Conclusion

Now you have the basics. **Universal Force Dynamics** is a language you can use to describe or analyze any kind of conflict or competition. Tactics instructors at the U.S. Army's Command and General Staff College, Fort Leavenworth, have used it to develop new tactics for the very complex Air/Land Battle doctrine. The Dallas Cowboys have used it as a language to teach movement through the line for linemen. Businessmen have used it to develop business strategies. Now lets see how it can be put to use for your purposes in the next chapter.

# CHAPTER 11

# TACTICS

Tactics for police and security officer combat situations are a little different than for the average street fight or a hand-to-hand fight on the battlefield. Because you have a certain amount of public trust placed upon you by the nature of your job, you have to be concerned about excessive force and appropriate levels of force. For this reason, the techniques used in this book are considerably milder than those presented in my previous books, Survival on the Battlefield: A Handbook to Military Martial Arts, Hapkido: The Integrated Fighting Art, and Surviving Hostage Situations. Most of the ones in this book involve just enough force to counter the attack and should be within the guidelines of justifiable force. The techniques in the earlier books include numerous ones that permanently maim or kill. How these security techniques are used in tactical combinations must also be governed by excessive force constraints. Given this reality, let's consider several aspects of close-quarters tactics.

## Attitude

Projecting the proper attitude can prevent a lot of trouble from ever starting. People who have a highly developed "street sense" know exactly what this is all about. Professional muggers, for instance, are careful as to whom they pick to mug. They can usually sense when a person has a lot of confidence. That self-confidence has to be based on something real, some ability that helps them feel safe. These people are usually left alone by muggers. Not long ago, I was returning from a training conference in Stuttgardt, West Germany. As I walked along in the train station carrying an overnight bag over my right shoulder and my overcoat over my right hand, I noticed a group of about fifteen scruffy, hippy-types standing off to the side. I didn't pay them much attention as this is a common sight in Europe. I walked by their group at a distance of about 30 feet. Out of the corner of my eye, I noticed a huge German youth detach himself from his group and rapidly walk toward me. Before a threat consciously registered in my mind and without thinking about why I was doing it, I glanced at him and transferred my coat to my left arm and clasped my bag's strap and continued to stride confidently along. His reaction was interesting. When he started toward me, he had been grinning. Suddenly he frowned, did an immediate about-face and rejoined his group. Looking back on the incident, I could see him spotting me as an easy mark. By appearances, I am an overweight, middle-aged Pilsbury Doughboy who walks with a limp (my knees have been destroyed by running and training accidents). From a distance he saw an easy mark. What changed his mind? At the same time that my security and combat instincts started operating, his did too. What he saw in me was a correct, automatic security response and enough confidence to keep on walking at the same pace with no apparent fear. In fact, I had already started to realize, at a conscious level, that he was getting ready to rip-off my bag and I was noting his stride so that I could select which of his knees I was going to break as he came in. Wasn't it nice that it all came to nothing. If I had stopped to confront him, he would probably have felt honor-bound to make the try or allow time for his friends to come in to help him. When I didn't stop, but just kept an eye on him, he probably determined it wasn't worth the risk. In this case, an unconscious attitude acquired over many years of experience prevented problems I didn't need.

As your training and experience increase, you too will start to exude an attitude of competency, one that may discourage trouble makers. Posturing, such as talking about what you're going to do or how bad you are, are invitations to a gun fight. **Cool calmness, direct eye contact, and smooth movements are far more intimidating than any bravado!**

# Belts of Security

As a physical security professional, you are an important link in a series of barriers/protective systems. In fact, you have equivalent belts or layers of security for your personal protection as well. Your sidearm is your furthest belt of protection. If you see a threat to life and property beyond your reach, your gun has the ability to reach out and neutralize or eliminate it. The next layer of security is your nightstick. It can reach beyond your hands to confront a threat. The third layer is closer in yet, your hands and feet. Finally, the closest belt and your last chance is to use close-range weapons such as elbows, knees, body, and head.

The idea is to try to identify the threat as far out as possible and use your longer-ranged weapons to eliminate it. The later the threat recognition, the shorter the range of weapon you'll be forced to employ and the greater the personal risk to yourself. The factors most important to successfully guarding yourself and your area of responsibility are **Battle-Awareness** and **Self-Awareness**. The true story used to illustrate the importance of attitude also illustrates this point. I was able to detect a potential threat at a long range which gave me the opportunity to increase my security precautions. I was able to ascertain my personal vulnerabilities in time to do something about them, switch the coat and clasp the bag's strap. If I hadn't been aware of what was going down and aware that my ability to respond was hampered, I could have lost my belongings.

# Water Theory

There are several Oriental fighting concepts that center around different aspects of water. These are:

- **Mind-Like-Water**

- **Mind-Like-Moon**

- **Water Pressure**

- **Water Influence**

- **Water Momentum**

Let's see how they play into close-quarters tactics for police and security forces.

**Mind-Like-Water:** This is a vital concept to many martial arts. The most effective mind in a combat situation is one that is totally free of emotion. It's free to focus its attention on the task at hand. Right away we can see its relationship to **UFD's concentration and conservation** of force factors. Ideally, your mind should be like a pool of water, totally placid and undisturbed. Allow one violent, uncontrolled emotion to enter the mind and it's as if a rock had been dropped into that placid pool. The whole surface becomes disturbed and concentration will be lost as a result. If you lose your concentration, you may also lose the **initiative**. People who have learned to do this become fighting machines, feeling no fear or pain until the combat has finished. They are capable of hearing and seeing more, moving faster and more powerfully, and sense reality as a slow motion film (which is called by another water name as being in the **"Flow State"**).

**Mind-Like-Moon:** Although not an aquatic name, this concept is completely intertwined with water theory and is essential for **Battle-Awareness**. You can only develop this ability if you have developed the **Mind-Like-Water** first. The moon bathes the landscape with a serene, all-knowing light. In the same manner, you must use your "soft eyes" and all your other senses to perceive everything happening around you. Eventually this be-

comes automatic. It's like having your own built-in radar. A good case in point was my sensing of danger in the train station without even being aware of it at first.

**Water Pressure:** Water exerts pressure on everything containing it and within it. You must learn to exert constant pressure on your assailant. Once he starts his assault, you must never let up the pressure on him. If you block / counter his attack, don't give him respite. Keep applying techniques until he is totally under control. Never give him a chance to regroup! You should always strive to anticipate the assailant's attack options and then limit them by combinations of **maneuver**, **tempo changes**, and **distancing**.

**Water Influence:** Water affects everything it touches by making them wet or by wearing them away. If an assailant wants to swim (to fight), he has to get wet (accept the consequences). You must learn to make his attacks so costly that he will think twice before trying it again. The way to do this is to create lots of pain and distress with your blocks and follow-up techniques. Most of the techniques in the earlier chapters of this book do just that.

**Water Momentum:** If a submarine springs a small leak, the pressure of the surrounding water will force itself into the small hole so hard that the hole will become larger and larger. In the same manner, you must look for an opening, attack it, and follow through with stronger and more effective techniques until the assailant is under control. Each technique opens a larger hole in his defenses until he's overwhelmed.

# Partners

Since many police and security personnel work in teams, you may have to fight that way. This sounds easy, but it isn't. Two or more people fighting on the same side can easily hinder each other's movements and accidently injure one another in the heat of battle. It is essential that you train as you fight. Practice double teaming an assailant in the gym before you try it on the street. Learn what each other's strengths and weaknesses are and decide ahead of time how you're going to mutually support one another. Develop a battle-drill signal system (both with words and signs) so you can communicate quickly and smoothly in battle.

It is best to use one partner as the initial combatant who blocks the attack and draws the assailant's attention so that the other partner can make an attempt to neutralize or control him. If both of you try to block / counter his attack simultaneously, you're likely to hinder each other. Assign specific roles to one another and practice them in "what if" situations in the gym so you do them automatically on the street. For instance, you might plan to go right every time your partner has to go left. This will insure that the attacker always ends up fighting a war on two fronts. The possibilities are endless and will keep your gym workouts interesting.

# Reinforcement

Notice that I keep saying, "In the gym do this. In the gym, do that." That implies that security and police officers should take the time to workout together. It doesn't have to be real elaborate, and it doesn't have to take up a lot of off-duty time, but do something! Once you've learned a few of these techniques, don't make the mistake of think-

ing you know it all. There's a lot of ways to fold, bend, spindle, and mutilate a body. Learning to deal with all the possible situations takes a lifetime.

Partners, don't think that the department or the company owes it to you to conduct all your training. **YOU OWE IT TO YOURSELVES TO GET AS GOOD AS YOU CAN AND KEEP THAT WAY! YOUR LIVES MAY DEPEND ON IT!** I can think of no better incentive to learn this business than that.

# Using UFD

The potential ways in which you can use **UFD** in battle are endless due to the incredible numbers of ways all the six principles and 22 factors can be combined. The best thing to do is experiment to find out what works best for you (again, you need to try this in the gym). To give you an idea of how this is done, I will describe a sequence of events using the language of **UFD**. If that helps you appreciate the sequence more, then try it out for yourself.

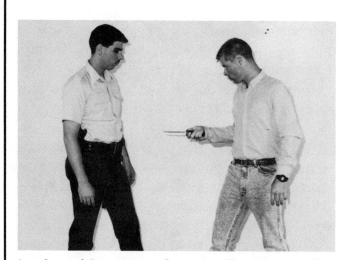

1. **At mid-range, the assailant <u>surprisingly</u> pulls a knife and commences to lunge at you.**

2. Because you had good <u>battle-awareness</u>, you see the threat as it develops. You jump back to <u>avoid</u> his initial force and....

3. Draw your nightstick to <u>concentrate</u> a <u>force-against-force</u> strike onto his wrist to take away his <u>initiative</u>.

4. As he drops the knife, you begin to <u>maneuver</u> to his outside where you take advantage of his poor relative <u>position</u> by...

5. Applying another <u>force-on-force</u> strike to his hamstring.

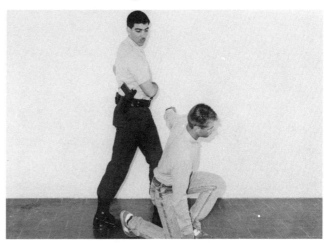

6. You then <u>coordinate</u> your <u>effort</u> by holstering your stick so that you are free to use your hands (<u>weapon selection</u>).

7. As he kneels in agony, you grab his wrist and neck to lock him up, insuring your <u>security</u> until your partner can <u>harmonize</u> his force with yours by cuffing the assailant.

Yes, I probably forced it a little; however, I wanted to prove that a sequence can be easily described using **UFD**. As you learn each of the techniques in this book, try to perceive them in this manner so that you will have a chance to use this language. Comfort with the language of **UFD** will, in turn, help you learn more techniques faster and better.

# INQUIRIES

We realize nothing is more frustrating than to get a taste of something and then have the meat taken away. Books like this, out of economic necessity, can never be truly complete. If they were, few people would buy them because of their vast size and cost.

We also realize that some of you have specific questions pertaining to your situations and programs. If you want to go deeper into this subject area or are with a law enforcement agency or security institution which needs assistance in setting up or expanding existing training programs, we suggest you contact Mr. Spear concerning his consulting schedule and practices. Make your inquiries to:

**UNIVERSAL FORCE DYNAMICS**
**410 DELAWARE**
**LEAVENWORTH, KS 66048**
**U.S.A.**
**(913) 682-6518**

# Universal Force Dynamics Publishing

Post Office Box 410, Leavenworth, KS
66048
(913) 682-6518, Fax (913) 651-0141

## 1994 Law Enforcement Catalog

FOR THE BEST IN FAMILY VALUES, MILITARY AND PERSONAL DEFENSE BOOKS AND TAPES. MAIL ORDER SERVICE FOR THE HOMESTEAD & SELF-RELIANCE MARKET. ADVERTISED REGULARLY IN MAJOR MEN'S MAGAZINES. BEST SELLING TITLES WITH DOUBLEDAY'S "MILITARY BOOK CLUB".

## ABOUT THE PUBLISHER ROBERT K. SPEAR

Robert K. Spear, a retired US Army Military Intelligence professional, has been training military and civilian personnel in self defense all over the world since 1974. A 6th degree black belt in Hapkido, Mr. Spear was selected as LTC James "Bo" Gritz's primary self defense and self reliance subject matter expert on his SPIKE (**S**pecially **P**repared **I**ndividuals for **K**ey **E**vents) training team. As a team member, he has trained over <u>8,000</u> people throughout the United States since June of 1993. **Col. Gritz believes Mr. Spear to be one of the top self defense trainers in the world because of his ability to teach proficiency to <u>anybody</u>— from young teenagers to eighty-year-old grandmothers!**

Bob Spear has been a popular instructor and lecturer for many years. His work shops have received rave reviews because they're easy, fun, and extremely effective. He is the author of seven books and numerous magazine articles, three self defense videos, and has appeared on radio talk shows all over America.

# UFD PUBLISHING PRESENTS THREE NEW VIDEO TAPE INSTRUCTION PROGRAMS

### Tape I ROBERT K. SPEAR TEACHES: DEFENSES AGAINST WEAPONS ATTACKS
- Unarmed defenses against knife attacks (3 people have been saved— a nurse from a patient's scissors attack, a husband from an assailant's knife & club attack, and a deputy sheriff from a prisoner's knife attack.)
- Unarmed defenses against stick and club attacks.
- Pistol take-aways.

### Tape II ROBERT K. SPEAR TEACHES: OFFENSIVE WEAPONS TECHNIQUES
- Knife fighting (1 young girl has been saved by her using the knife Mr. Spear recommends against a male assailant in a highway rest area's bathroom (she didn't even have to injure him)).
- Nightstick and extendable ASP baton.
- Billy club and flashlight.
- Walking canes.
- Making padded training aids.

### Tape III ROBERT K. SPEAR TEACHES: FIGHTING UP CLOSE AND IN CONFINED SPACES
- Releases from holds and chokes.
- Applying come-alongs.
- Frisks and escaping from frisks.
- Fighting on the ground (85% of street fights end up rolling around on the ground).
- Fighting while up against walls and in corners.
- Fighting from a chair or while in your automobile.

Tapes retail for $40.00 each, or preferably, get them as a set of three for $100.00.
**Doubleday's Military Book Club has already decided to include these in their next Christmas catalog because they have sold so many of Mr. Spear's military self defense books.**

# UFD PERSONAL SECURITY BOOKS

**04/D Close Quarters Combat for Police and Security Forces** by Robert K. Spear

Controlling, containment, and baton techniques for common street threats. Subjects include: proper use of night stick, come-alongs, unarmed attacks, knife attacks, club attacks, pistol disarming, ground fighting, training aids and drills, martial art theory, and tactics.
ISBN: 0-9622627-4-9, 128 pages, 350 photos, 8.5 x 11 pbk, **$19.95**.

**05/D Survival On the Battlefield: A Handbook to Military Martial Arts** by Robert K. Spear
Complete training program for killing and maiming techniques. Subjects include theory, body weapons, kicks, breakfalls, throws, chokes, locks, come-alongs; defenses against— strikes, clubs, knives, bayonets, chokes, kicks, throws, holds & grabs; ground fighting; knife fighting; sentry neutralization; expedient weapons; training female soldiers, the Threat's training, physical and mental conditioning, training facilities & aids, drills, programs, and teaching tactics and strategies.
ISBN: 0-86568-093-0, 190 pages, 350 photos, pbk, **$14.95**.

**06/D Military Knife Fighting** by Robert K. Spear
Great basic book. Subjects include: Fighting grips and stances, targets, blocks and counters, serial and parallel attacks, knife grappling, sentry kills, knife vs bayonet, knife vs entrenching tool, knife throwing, & training hints. ISBN: 0-9622627-6-5, 126 pages, 120 photos, 5.5 x 8.5 pbk, **$9.95**

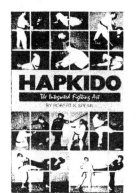

**07/D Hapkido: The Integrated Fighting Art** by Robert K. Spear, 6th Dan, U.S. Hapkido Federation.
An overview of Mr. Spear's art. Subjects include: history, philosophy, training, belt system, warm-up & cool-down exercises, basic kicks and strikes, breakfalls, joint locks, sweeps, basic and advanced kick and punch defenses, escapes, free sparring, cane and fighting stick techniques.
ISBN: 0-86568-079-5, 186 pages, 350 photos, 8.5 x 11 pbk, **$12.95**.

**11/P Surviving Hostage Situations** by Robert K. Spear and LTC D. Michael Moak
Most of us don't like to think about bad things which might happen to us. But, what would you do if you walked into a convenience store while it was being robbed and found yourself in a hostage situation? This primer covers: the hostage takers, hostage situations, emotional / psychological expectations, coping with captivity, planning an escape, physical resistance, executing an escape, rescue— who and what to expect, getting back to normal, how to prepare the family, recommendation for survival, and a family contingency plan. Translated into German, and a steady seller in English all over the world, this book has helped many victims.
ISBN: 0-9622627-5-7, 144 pages, 60 illustrations, 8.5 x 11 pbk, **$14.95**.

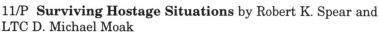

# FIELD FIGHTER KNIVES

The **Field Fighter** design was named Fighting Knife pick of the year by **Fighting Knives Magazine** in 1992. It is prominently featured in Rick Marcinko and John Weisman's **Rogue Warrior Red Cell** novel series. The **Field Fighter** is one of the few knives designed specifically for both punishing field and camping work, as well as an awesome fighting knife. Each knife is hand made by the Stone Mountain Hatchet Works in Arkansas so allow 120 days for delivery. Believe us, the wait will be worth it! This is the only big knife you will ever need! Each knife comes with a copy of Robert K. Spear's **Military Knife Fighting** manual.

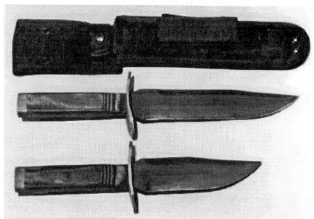

**209/W Field Fighter I:** 9.5" blade made from spring steel with its edges selectively hardened to a Rockwell 58. This makes for super sharp, durable edges yet the blade, as a whole, will take an incredible amount of punishment. The knife's balance is forward to allow for better hacking and slashing. The front third of the blade is double edged. The mat-black finish insures no telltale reflections. A grainy micarta handle makes for a sure grip, while a very large brass guard provides superlative protection for the fingers and hand. Blade-catching notches increase the opportunities for wrenching an opponent's knife out of his hands. The custom designed balistic nylon sheath with a kydex liner produced by Eagle Industries is structured for quick release from a pistol belt or to be hung from any position on your web gear. **$190 plus $6.00 S&H.**

**210/W Field Fighter II:** 6" blade and slightly downsized handle make for a more compact knife without sacrificing any of its strengths. This is ideal for pilots & armored vehicle drivers who have limited room for equipment, or for people with smaller hands who may be uncomfortable with too big a knife. **$180.00 plus $6.00 S&H**.

**Robert K. Spear is available for workshops and seminars. For information call: (913) 651-0141 or (913) 682-6518, or write to us at UFD Publishing, POB 410, Leavenworth, KS 66048..**

# ORDER FORM
### Universal Force Dynamics Publishing, POB 410, Leavenworth, KS 66048

| QTY | ITEM | PRICE EA | TOTAL PRICE |
|---|---|---|---|
| | Video Tape 1 | 40.00 | |
| | Video Tape 2 | 40.00 | |
| | Video Tape 3 | 40.00 | |
| | Video Tape Set (all Three) | 100.00 | |
| | Close Quarters Cbt for Police | 19.95 | |
| | Survival on the Battlefield | 14.95 | |
| | Military Knife Fighting | 9.95 | |
| | Hapkido | 12.95 | |
| | Surviving Hostage Situations | 14.95 | |
| | Field Fighter I | 190.00 | |
| | Field Fighter II | 180.00 | |
| | | Subtotal | |
| | | Less Dealer Discount | |
| | | Subtotal | |
| | | Tax (KS only) | |
| | | S&H | |
| | | Total | |

**Dealer & Organizational Discounts:** 10 - 99 books = 40%, 100+ = 50% discounts. Book and video S&H $3.00 total cost, Knives $6.00 each.

PO #: _____

Name / Company: _____

Address: _____

City: _____

State: _____ Zip: _____

Country: _____

Telephone: _____